DISCOVERING
GREAT
Artists

Hands-On Art for Children
in the Styles of the Great Masters

MaryAnn F. Kohl

Kim Solga

illustrations
Rebecca Van Slyke

BRIGHT IDEAS
FOR LEARNING

Bright Ring
Publishing, Inc.

CREDITS

Illustrations	Rebecca Van Slyke
Artist Portraits	Kim Solga
Typography	textype, Trish Lemon, Dorothy Tjoelker-Worthen
Cover Design	MaryAnn Kohl
Cover Illustration	Christina Critelli, age 6
Back Cover	Trish Lemon, Joe Shahan

ISBN 0-935607-09-9

Library of Congress Catalog Card Number: 97-71761

Manufactured in the United States of America   First Printing May 1997

Attention: Schools and Businesses

Bright Ring Publishing, Inc.'s books are available for quantity discounts with bulk purchase for educational, business, or sales promotion use. Please contact:

Bright Ring Publishing, Inc.
P.O. Box 31338
Bellingham, WA 98228-3338
800-480-4278 • www.brightring.com

Publisher's Cataloging in Publication Data

Kohl, MaryAnn F.
   Discovering great artists : hands-on art for children in the styles of the great masters / MaryAnn F. Kohl, Kim Solga; illustrations, Rebecca Van Slyke.
      p. cm. – (Bright ideas for learning)
   Includes indexes
   ISBN: 0-935607-09-9
SUMMARY: Approximately 80 visual artists, from Giotto to Van Allsburg, are featured in this collective biography, which also includes instructions for art projects which correspond to each artist's style or technique.
      1. Artists – Biography – Juvenile literature.   2. Art – Technique – Juvenile literature.   I. Solga, Kim.   II. Title.   III. Series.
N42.K64 1997   709.2'2'024054
                                                               QBI97-40470

DEDICATIONS

In memory of my parents, Jay and Betty Faubion, who read to me every night of my childhood. - MAK

To Nici, who was always willing to try out an art project for her mom. - KS

ACKNOWLEDGMENTS

Deepest gratitude and praise to the young great artists who contributed to this book with their original works of art:

Aaron Avsshai, age 12, Lake and Sky Watercolor

Amanda Schwittay, age 7, Woven Mat

Amy King, age 7, Girl Portrait

Ashley Cole, age 6, Tesselating Puppy, inspired by a tessela from Dale Seymour Publications

Chad Noward, age 7, Squirrel

Christina Critelli, age 6, Bridge

Christina Critelli, age 6, Starry Night

David Royce, age 7, Paper Collage

Davin LaRue, age 5, Paper Shapes

Geneva Faulkner, age 8, Mother, Baby & Angels, and Self Portrait

Hannah Kohl, ages 6-8, Queen, Wagon and Pig, and One-Line Cat and House

Jackie Lemon, age 9, Tree House

Jacob Aiello, age 8, Baseball Box

Jared Lollar, age 8, Invasion from Mars

Jenny Lemon, age 7, Chomp, and Wiggly Watercolor Design

Jesse Pennington, age 11, Foil Duck

Jesse Vander Hoek, age 8, Facial Expressions

Jodi Drost, age 9, Quilt Scene, and Winter Barn

Jordan Drost, age 10, Dancing Cow, and Ladder Chair

Katherine Shelley, age 8, Asthma Camp

Katie Rodriguez, age 8, Girl's Profile

Kim Dettman, age 12, Cloudy Sky

Kim Solga, Student Art

Kyle Casteel, age 8, Birthday Poster

Madeline Vander Pol, age 7, Dog Feeder

Matt Means, age 8, smiling boy in photograph

Megan Kohl, age 7, Sunset

Melinda de Bruin, age 8, "You&Me" Picture

Morgan Van Slyke, age 1, Paper Collage

Nici Smith, ages 9-12, Chalk Fish, Robot Collage, Wire Man, Cowboy Sculpture, Desert Watercolor, Watercolor Flower, Horse of Dots

Peter James, age 7, Jungle

Rob Harweger, age 8, Gallery Picture

Ryan Phillips, age 12, Name Plaque

Sally Ann Mitchell, age 6, Egg Flowers

Scott Brandl, age 8, Loon

Tara McKinney, age 8, Pitcher with Flowers

Tatiana Huaracha, age 8, Camping Picnic, and Dinosasur with Foil

Thanks to Fred W. Smith, Mt. Shasta, California, for his photography throughout the book.

Original art of the following artists is used with permission from Planet Art CD ROM Royalty Free Graphics, Beverly Hills, California:

Dürer, Rhinoceros, 1500

Kahlo, c. 1940, Self-Portrait

Limbourg Brothers, 1413, Tres Riches Heures

Linnaeus, c. 1760, Sunflower

Magritte, c. 1950

Michelangelo, 1512, Father God

Raphael, 1510, Madonna della Sectia

Rembrandt, 1642, Night Watch

Rivera, c. 1945

Toulouse-Lautrec, 1891, Moulin Rouge La Goulue

Van Gogh, 1888, Sunflowers

"A man paints with his brains and not with his hands."
- Michelangelo

Introduction

Discovering Great Artists **offers children hands-on activities to explore the styles and techniques of the world's greatest artists.** Each art process focuses on one style and one artist. A brief biography and portrait of each artist adds depth and interest to the art project. The most important aspects of the art projects are discovery, exploration, and individual creativity. The finished product will be an indirect benefit.

Discovering Great Artists **introduces children to the great masters.** Many great artists will be familiar names, like Michelangelo, da Vinci, Picasso, Rembrandt and van Gogh. Other names will perhaps be new, such as Arp, Nevelson, Hokusai, or Paik. Each featured artist has a style that is readily imitated and explored by children, with a life history that will inspire or add depth to the experience. Try one or try them all!

Discovering Great Artists **is a book of exploring.** Young children are usually most interested in the process of art, not the finished product, and may or may not show interest in the associated art history or art appreciation. Many will be curious and can absorb as much as their interests allow. Most older children will want to know more about the artist's life and how it affected the artist's style. No one is required to learn the history of each artist or the eras or movements they represent. The information on each page is offered as a source of reference and inspiration for interested learners. Don't be surprised if children want to collect information about different artists much the way they collect baseball cards and statistics.

Discovering Great Artists **encourages children to learn by doing, to become familiar with new ideas.** If a child experiences painting with the impasto paint van Gogh used in his swirling, expressive brushstrokes, then that child will feel more comfortable and familiar as an older student or adult studying van Gogh. Imagine visiting a gallery in Paris and seeing that same impasto style by van Gogh in person! Many children have expressed that it is like meeting an old friend.

The most important thing for the child is to explore new art ideas and techniques. Above all, the activities are "open-ended". It is up to the child to decide exactly how his or her work of art will turn out. Independent thinking is encouraged, while skills and responsibility are enhanced through individual decisions.

Discovering Great Artists **offers art activities to expand the creative experience and awareness of children in all aspects of the visual arts through:** painting, drawing, printing, sculpture, architecture, and other manipulations of art materials. The activities in this book work well for all ages and abilities, from the most basic skill level to the most challenging. Repeat projects often and see new outcomes and learnings each time.

Discovering Great Artists **encourages children to expand their knowledge.** Getting to know great artists will inspire children to read books, visit museums, go to the library, collect information, and look at the world in a new way. They will begin to encompass a greater sense of history and art appreciation and see themselves in the scope of time. Perhaps they will be inspired to carry art in their hearts as they grow and develop. They are already great artists in every sense of the word.

Art Resources

Resources for wonderful art materials are everywhere you look – in libraries, in stores, in museum shops, in catalogs, in the trash! Once you start looking, they will seem to appear out of nowhere! Some are free while others range from inexpensive to costly.

Books with colorful reproductions of artwork are readily available at libraries and bookstores. Posters and prints of famous artwork can be purchased from catalogs, bookstores, museum shops, or checked out from most libraries. Illustrations can be cut out of magazines and used books, then mounted on cardboard to create small posters and cards. Many videos and slide sets are available for school and home use. The internet offers connections with museums around the world, with thousands of great paintings to view. Visits to museums, art galleries and the studios of local artists, give children eyewitness, hands-on experiences with works of art. Free brochures and catalogs of expensive art prints can be cut apart and used in many ways. The following resources for books, prints and other art history materials are suggested. Contact all of them for their free brochures and catalogs.

BOOKS ABOUT ARTISTS FOR CHILDREN

- *Eyewitness Art, series*
  by Colin Wiggins
  Over 10 books. Like having a private art gallery or museum. Available on Perspective, Watercolor, Monet, Manet, Goya, Renaissance, and more. Post Impressionism is excellent.
  Published by Dorling Kindersley, Inc., New York, NY
  Look at other publications by Dorling Kindersley.
- *The Famous Artists, series*
  Offers 8 excellent paperback books on famous artists, including Miro, Da Vinci, Michelangelo. Many others.
  Published by Barrons Education Series, Inc., Hauppauge, NY
- *The First Impressions, series*
  Offers at least 17 titles developed especially for young people (and old people who like things simple and sweet!), with each artist's own works and life story. Titles include: Chagall, Cassatt, Frank Lloyd Wright, Rembrandt, Wyeth. Many more.
  Published by Harry N. Abrams, Inc., New York, NY
- *Getting to Know the World's Greatest Artists, series*
  by Mike Venezia
  Gives children a delightful glimpse into the lives of 13 different artists and their works.
  Published by Children's Press, Chicago, IL

- *Mommy, It's A Renoir, series*
  Provides a system of games and activities that teach children about great artists and their paintings.
  Published by Parent Child Press, Hollidaysburg, PA
- *Talking With Artists*
  by Pat Cummings
  Conversations with 14 favorite children's book illustrators including Chris Van Allsburg, *The Polar Express.*
  Published by Bradbury Press, New York, NY
- *Weekend with Picasso, series*
  Just one of the titles in an interesting series of stories with imaginary visits to great artist's studios.
  Published by Skira/Rizzoli, New York, NY
- *Women Artists for Children, series*
  Offers a special focus on the life and techniques of several great artists, including O'Keeffe, Kahlo, and Casatt.
  Published by Little, Brown, and Co., Boston, MA

POSTERS AND ART PRINTS
Write to each supplier for a catalog, price, and availability. Many of the catalogs will be sources for cut-and-paste activities using prints of great art.

Prints, Posters, and Laminated Reproductions
- Art Extension Press, Box 389, Westport, CT 06881
  Dover Publications (Print Portfolios), 31 East 2nd St., Mineola, NY 11501
- Parent Child Press (Art Prints for Children), PO Box 675, Hollidaysburg, PA 16648
- Shorewood Reproductions, 27 Glen Rd., Sandy Hook, CT 06482
- University Prints, 21 East St., Winchester, MA 02890

Postcard Art Reproductions
- Abbeybille Press, Inc., 488 Madison Avenue, New York, NY 10022
- Dover Publications - see above
- Parent Child Press (*Mommy, It's A Renoir* materials) see books above
- Pavilion Books Limited, 196 Shaftesbury Avenue, London WC2H 8JL, England
- Running Press, 125 S. 2nd St., Philadelphia, PA 19103

Programs, Textbooks, Newsletters, and Other Books
- Art Image Publications, PO Box 568, Champlain, NY 12919
- Art Media, Etc., 1905 Studebaker Pl., Gold River, CA 95670

- Bright Ideas for Learning, series, art activity books by MaryAnn F. Kohl, Bright Ring Publishing, Inc., PO Box 31338, Bellingham, WA 98228-3338
- Crizmac, PO Box 65928, Tucson, AZ 85728
- KidsArt, art education booklets, PO Box 274, Mt. Shasta, CA 96067
- Dale Seymour, PO Box 10888, Palo Alto, CA 94303
- Davis Publications, 50 Portland St., Worcester, MA 01608
- Wilton Programs, PO Box 541, Wilton, CT 06897

Museum Reproductions
- Metropolitan Museum of Art, Special Services Office, Middle Village, NY 11381
- Museum of Fine Arts, PO Box 1044, Boston, MA 02120
- Museum of Modern Art, 11 West 53rd St., New York, NY 10019
- National Gallery of Art, Publications Services, 2000 B. South Club Dr., Landover, MD 20785
- St. Louis Art Museum, Resource Center, Forest Park, St. Louis, MO 63110-1380
- Whitney Museum of Art, 945 Madison Ave., New York, NY 10021
- museum gift stores
- all local art galleries and museums with art

THE INTERNET
- Museums and galleries around the world have sites on the internet, with more added each month. This is a new and changing medium. Our best recommendation is to use a search option to find names of individual artists or museums. These searches will yield the most current information, and by following the links suggested, a world of information and images will be discovered.

DON'T FORGET
- The public library has the most to offer for children's curiosity, found both in the children's and the adult departments. Enjoy the discovery of searching for materials to supplement *Discovering Great Artists* based on the curiosity of each individual child.
- Free catalogs are available from museums and museum shops, filled with reproductions of great art that can be cut apart to your heart's content!

Icons

Positioned in the upper right corner of each art activity page are icons which help the parent, teacher, or young artist select a particular project as to any of the following:

EXPERIENCE LEVEL

Assists in choosing, not limiting, choices of art experiences, with stars to indicate difficulty, and if adult supervision may be helpful.

 EASY- BEGINNING
artists with little art experience

 MODERATE-INTERMEDIATE
artists with some art experience and skill

 INVOLVED-EXPERIENCED
artists with a variety of art experiences and practice

Age and skill do not necessarily go hand and hand. Therefore, the "experience icon" flags the projects most appropriate for new or beginning-level artists, mid-level artists with some experience, or advanced-level artists with greater experience who work more independently. However, all children can explore all projects whether the skill level matches their own or not - they may simply need a little more time to work or extra help with difficult steps. And remember, most experienced artists will also enjoy the easier levels, too.

ART TECHNIQUE

Shows what art medium or technique is utilized in the project.

 PAINT/DYE

 SCULPT

 PRINT

 CUT/CONSTRUCT

 DRAW/COLOR

 GAMES/ACTIVITIES

 CHALK

PLANNING AND PREPARATION

Indicates the degree of involvement and planning time for the adult in charge.

 EASY

 MODERATE

 INVOLVED

Icons continued

ARTIST STYLE

Great artists from the past and present are often grouped into descriptive movements, styles, or eras. These are described in more detail in Chapter 6, under Great Art Words p.132-138. Some artists are found grouped under more than one style and still others are difficult to place in any one particular style. The more that artists and their techniques are explored, the easier it is to see how they fit into categories. Don't expect to know this all at once! It can take years of enjoyment, discovery, and study. For now, they are presented for the curious-minded who wish to know more and to help categorize the unique styles of each great artist.

 ABSTRACT

 ABSTRACT-EXPRESSIONISM

 BAROQUE

 CARTOON

 CHILDREN'S BOOK ILLUSTRATOR

 CUBISM

 EXPRESSIONISM

 FOLK ART

 GOTHIC

 IMPRESSIONISM

 MODERN

 NATURALISM

 OP AND POP ART

 PHOTOJOURNALISM

 POST IMPRESSIONISM

 REALISM

 RENAISSANCE

 ROMANTICISM

 SURREALISM

 UKIYO-E (EDO PERIOD)

Chart of Contents

LONG, LONG AGO

chapter 1

Renaissance &
Post Renaissance

Scott Brandl, age 8, Loon in a Circle

Giotto 1266-1337

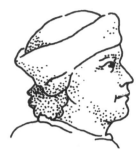

Giotto di Bondone

When Giotto was a young boy tending sheep in the mountains of northern Italy, he drew pictures to help pass the time. A traveling artist discovered Giotto's drawings and offered him an apprenticeship. There Giotto learned how to make paintbrushes and art tools, which minerals could be used to create different colors of paint, and worked on drawings and small parts of paintings. Eventually Giotto left to find work on his own. He became the chief master of cathedral building and public art in Florence, Italy. Giotto is best known for painting people who appeared three-dimensional rather than flat.

Many paintings of Giotto's time were made with egg tempera paint on special panels of wood. There were no art stores, so each artist had to make paint by grinding minerals, clay, berries, or even insects into fine powder and mixing this pigment with egg yolk and water. Egg tempera makes a thin, fast drying coat of bright color. The paint is very strong and long lasting. Giotto's beautiful egg tempera paintings are over 700 years old!

Young artists explore Giotto's technique of painting with egg tempera with a homemade recipe made with crushed chalk.

Giotto's (ZHEE-O-TO) paints were made from egg yolks mixed with clay, minerals, berries, or even ground insects to make colored pigments.

Egg Paint

MATERIALS
- colored chalk (bright pastel chalk works best)
- muffin tin, plastic egg carton, or paint palette for mixing
- egg and some water
- spoon and a fork
- old bowl
- round rock
- paintbrush and paper

PROCESS
1. Break off small pieces of colored chalk and grind them into powder in an old bowl with a round rock. Note: Avoid breathing the chalk powder.
2. Put the colored powders into the cups of a muffin tin, egg carton or paint palette.
3. Crack the egg and separate the yellow yoke from the clear egg white.
4. Put the yolk in a clean bowl and mix it with 2 teaspoons of water. Whip it with a fork until the mixture is frothy yellow.
5. Add spoons of egg-water to the powdered chalk and stir with a paintbrush until you make a smooth, runny paint.
6. Now use the egg tempera paint to make a painting!

Sally Ann Mitchell, age 6, Egg Flowers

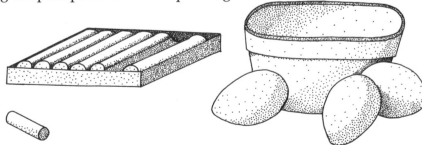

Limbourg Brothers 1375-1416

*The Limbourg Brothers (**LIHM**-BORG) – Paul, Herman, and Jean – created incredibly detailed paintings for a calendar using tiny paintbrushes and magnifying lenses.*

Book of Days

MATERIALS
- paper
- pencil, eraser, and ruler
- photocopy machine
- colored marking pens, colored pencils, or crayons
- magnifying glass
- 2 sheets of heavy paper as covers
- stapler or hole punch and yarn

PROCESS
1. Design a layout for the pages of the Book of Days. The Limbourg Brothers used a square topped by a half circle. Draw these shapes on a piece of paper with a pencil and ruler, or invent other shapes to frame the drawings that will be made. When the design is ready, draw over the pencil lines with a black marker.
2. Photocopy the page design. Make 4 copies, one for each season of the year, or make 12 copies, one for each month. Save the original page design to make copies later, if desired.
3. Draw a picture on each of the photocopy pages. Pick a favorite thing about each season or month. Perhaps draw a holiday or sport or how the neighborhood looks at that time of year. Put lots of little details into each drawing, just like The Limbourg Brothers did hundred of years ago. Use a magnifying lens to see the details close up. Write the name of the season or month in the border of each picture.
4. Fasten the drawings together with 2 sheets of heavy paper as covers. Staple them together or use a hole punch with yarn ties to bind the Book of Days.

The Limbourg Brothers

One of the most beautiful works of art from the middle ages is a book of paintings made by three men known as The Limbourg Brothers. This is a book called the Tres Riches Heures. *The brothers Paul, Herman, and Jean were hired by the rich nobleman, Duc de Berry, to create a book with a calendar, lists of the holy days, and prayers and pictures of the seasons. They did this incredibly detailed creation with paints they made themselves using tiny paintbrushes and magnifying lenses to add detail.*

Young artists create a "Book of Days" by drawing calendar pictures of the artist's favorite times of the year.

Limbourg Brothers,
Tres Riches Heures, 1413

Ghiberti 1378-1455

Lorenzo Ghiberti

In the year 1401, the city of Florence, Italy held a competition to choose an artist to decorate the doors of the beautiful city church. The winner was a young sculptor named Lorenzo Ghiberti. He created a scene from the Bible, with figures that rose up out of the background. Ghiberti had been trained as a goldsmith, and the shimmer of his gold-plated bronze delighted the judges. They liked Ghiberti's calm, elegant people with their softly flowing robes.

Ghiberti worked all of his life on the great Baptistery doors at Florence. Many artists worked under him, carving the scenes, casting the metal panels, and covering them with pure gold. It took 20 years to finish the first set of doors — then the city hired Ghiberti to make even more. Michelangelo later said of Ghiberti's baptistery doors, "They are worthy to stand at the Gates of Paradise."

Young artists create a relief panel using cardboard, string, glue, and aluminum foil to explore the style of Ghiberti, and it won't take nearly so long to complete!

*Michelangelo said of Ghiberti's (GHEE-**BAIR**-TEE) creation of shimmering gold baptistery doors, "They are worthy to stand at the Gates of Paradise."*

Florentine Relief

MATERIALS

- piece of cardboard, 6" square or larger
- matte board and heavy paper scraps
- heavy string, yarn or twine
- white glue
- scissors
- heavy duty aluminum foil
- tape
- black ink or tempera paint and a paintbrush
- steel wool
- sheet of colored construction paper

PROCESS

1. Cut some shapes out of the matte board and heavy paper. Glue these shapes onto the cardboard sheet.
2. Glue some string down.
3. Lay a sheet of foil over everything. The foil should be larger than the piece of cardboard so the foil edges hang over the cardboard edges. Gently press the foil down onto the design. Press and rub all over so the shapes and textures of the paper and string show through the foil. Fold the foil edges to the back of the cardboard and tape them down.
4. With scrap newspaper underneath, paint the entire foil surface with black ink or tempera paint. Let everything dry overnight.
5. The next day, rub the surface of the foil gently with steel wool to shine up the high spots. Leave the dark ink or paint in the low spots.
6. Glue the relief design onto a larger sheet of construction paper.

Jesse Pennington, age 11, Foil Duck

Van Eyck 1395-1441

*Over five hundred years ago in the 1400's Jan van Eyck (VAN **IKE**) was the most famous painter of northern Europe and was said to be the inventor of oil paints.*

Triptych Panel

MATERIALS
- white cardboard, foam board or stiff paper
- ruler and pencil
- scissors or an adult helper with a craft knife
- watercolors or tempera for painting
- roll of dark colored duct tape or wide masking tape
- markers, crayons, or colored pencils for drawing

PROCESS
1. A triptych has three panels as shown in the illustration: one wide panel in the center, and two narrower side pieces that can fold over the center one. The tops are often rounded. It's easy to make a cardboard triptych by measuring and cutting two identical center pieces, rectangles with rounded tops. Then cut one of these pieces straight down the middle to make the two narrow side panels. (See illustration.)
2. Place the cut panel on top of the whole panel and tape the outside edges. Now, with the tape as a hinge, stand the cardboard up and fold them open. Add more tape on the inside, if needed, or tape all around the panels to create a frame, if desired.
3. Now the fun begins. Design a scene on the open faces of the triptych. For example, draw a picture in the middle with two smaller pictures on the side panels. Or make one large picture that goes across all three panels. The decision is the artist's. Sketch the picture.
4. Next color or paint the scene or picture on the panels. Dry completely.
5. When the center picture is finished and dry, fold the side panels over the middle and there will be another surface to decorate! Draw and color, or paint a picture on the two outside panels of the triptych. Dry completely.
6. Display the triptych in a home or classroom on a table or shelf. Leave it closed with just the outside pictures showing most of the time. Then, on special days, open it up for the full inside scene!

Jan van Eyck

Jan van Eyck was the most famous painter of northern Europe in the 1400's, over five hundred years ago. For many years, he was said to be the inventor of oil paints; although he didn't actually invent mixing pigments with oil to make paint, van Eyck was the first artist to really master this new material.
Unlike egg tempera paints used in earlier times, oil paints could be applied in thick coats or in very thin glazes and could create rich, velvety colors that seemed to glow from within. Van Eyck was a master oil painter. He painted religious scenes, portraits of wealthy people, and even pictures of himself.

One of van Eyck's most famous paintings is an altar piece called a triptych, which is a wood framed screen made in three parts. There are pictures on the outside of the screen when it is folded shut, and more on the inside when it is opened up. Young artists can create a triptych panel out of stiff paper or cardboard, drawing pictures to decorate both its open and closed surfaces.

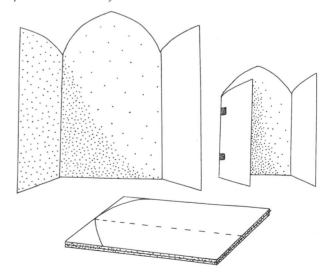

Angelico 1400-1455

Fra Giovanni Angelico

Fra Angelico da Fiesoie was an Italian monk who was one of the greatest painters of the early Renaissance. Fra was not his name—it was his title in the monastery, meaning "brother", like being called Mr. or Dr.

Fra Angelico learned drawing and painting by illuminating manuscripts at the monastery, hand lettering pages of books, and drawing pictures to illustrate stories. He was asked to paint on the walls of his monastery, fresco paintings made on wet new white plaster. Angelico painted inspiring scenes from the Christian Bible. His pictures are very beautiful, filled with delicate colors and a feeling of peaceful serenity.

Artists of this era often gave halos to the angels and people in their paintings. This golden ring around a figure's head was meant to show an inner goodness shining out for everyone to see. Halos were often made with real gold, not with gold paint. Gold metal was pounded into a very thin sheet called "gold leaf", then glued onto the wall or canvas with varnish. Young artists paint beautiful pictures with "silver leaf" decoration using everyday aluminum foil.

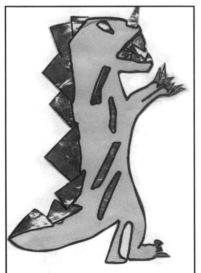

Tatiana Huaracha, age 8,
Dinosaur with Foil

Fra Angelico (AHN-**JEH**-LIH-KO) painted golden halos around a person's head to show an inner goodness shining out for everyone to see. Halos were often made with real gold, not with gold paint.

Painting with Silver Leaf

MATERIALS

- construction paper, dark sheet
- pencil or chalk for sketching
- aluminum foil
- scissors
- white glue
- tempera paints and brushes

PROCESS

1. Choose a dark color of construction paper for this project, such as -
   rich purple   black   midnight blue   red
2. Sketch a large design on the paper with the pencil. Draw the face of an angel, like Fra Angelico, or draw any other subject desired, such as -
   a fish with shiny silver scales
   a crown with jewels
   a robot from outer space
   an abstract design of foil and color
3. Next, cut pieces of aluminum foil to fit some of the areas in the drawing and glue them down. For example, on a fish design, the head, fins and tail could be shiny silver foil. For an angel design, a silver halo would be effective. For a robot design, foil parts of the head and body and buttons to push. Use imagination to select the foil areas.
4. Paint around the shiny foil pieces with tempera paints. Outline the foil, if desired, but try not to get too much paint on the shiny sliver areas. The foil should look like a jewel glittering against the colorful paint and dark background of the paper.

VARIATION

- There are many kinds of shiny metallic paints that are fun for kids to use in their paintings and designs. Gold and silver tempera, metallic acrylic, metallic printmaking ink (the water-soluble kind) and even gold and silver marking pens are available. Good sources are school supply stores or art supply stores. Choose materials that are child-safe and non-toxic.

Masaccio 1401-1428

Masaccio (MAH-SAH-CHEE-O) liked to add fancy details in his portrait paintings, such as hats, jewelry, and highly ornate decor.

Profile Portrait

MATERIALS

- slide or overhead projector
- white paper
- masking tape
- pencils, crayons, pens
- glue, optional
- two people: one the model, one the artist
- paints and brushes
- matte board scraps for framing, optional

PROCESS

1. Ask a friend to model for this side-profile portrait. The model should stand near a blank wall, standing so he is facing sideways.

2. With adult help, shine a slide projector or other bright light on the model so the shadow falls on the wall. Tape a sheet of white paper to the wall to catch the shadow of the model's head and shoulders. Trace the shape of the model's face and head, neck, and shoulders with the pencil. Then turn off the bright light, and move the paper from the wall to the work table.

3. For a realistic portrait, ask the model to sit down beside the work table so the artist can look at the model's features while painting or drawing. If the portrait is going to be more imaginary, the model may no longer be needed.

4. With paints and brushes or other drawing tools, add facial features to the pencil portrait, such as eyes, eyebrows, mouth, ears, and hair. Paint or color-in the further details of the model (or of an imaginary person such as a princess, clown, alien from outer space, or other character).

5. Add other ornate ideas and details too, such as, a hat, jewelry, glasses, fancy clothing, background wallpaper, and so on. Dry the profile portrait overnight. Note: Sometimes it is necessary to let some of the details painted dry a little between applications so they don't run together, if the artist is concerned about this. Otherwise, the running together of paints and colors can be artistically pleasing too. Or, use colored markers to avoid drying time.

6. To frame, go to a framing store and ask for framing scraps or matte board scraps. Glue these around the portrait, if desired, to frame.

Tommasso Masaccio

Masaccio is famous for his portraits during the Renaissance Period in art, a time when new ideas and new ways of thinking were just awakening. Masaccio liked to add fancy details in his portrait paintings, such as hats, jewelry, and highly ornate decor. Portraits can be drawn or painted in many ways, but the approach used in Profile Portrait assures the perfect full side view of a person's face, just like Masaccio enjoyed painting. Adding an abundance of detail and decoratives helps the young artist paint the way the great Renaissance artist, Masaccio, painted portraits.

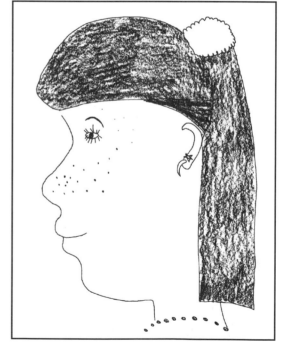

Katie Rodriquez, age 8, Girl's Profile

Botticelli 1445-1510

Sandro Botticelli

The early Renaissance artist Alessandro Filipepi was born in the Italian city of Florence where many painters lived and worked. He changed his name to Botticelli after he became a professional artist. Like most artists of this era, Botticelli was apprenticed when he was still a young boy and lived at the studio of his master, a goldsmith, along with the other young apprentices. Here he learned to do all the jobs of the artist.

Botticelli worked for the rich and powerful patrons, the Medici family. As part of what Botticelli owed his patrons, he painted many portraits of the the Medici family. He also created religious paintings and scenes from Roman mythology for them.

Botticelli is well known for the many round compositions he created, a popular shape for paintings in his day. Young artists drawing in a circle, creating "art in the round".

Scott Brandl, age 8,
Loon in a Circle

*In the days of Botticelli (BAH-TUH-**CHEL**-LAY), round paintings were a new and popular idea in works of art.*

Art in the Round

MATERIALS

- large sheets of white drawing paper, textured papers, construction paper
- scissors
- large bowl, plate or pizza pan
- smaller round objects like saucers and jar lids
- markers, crayons or pencils for drawing
- any paints and paintbrushes

PROCESS

1. Art paper usually comes in square or rectangular sheets. So young artists must first make their own pads of round paper for painting or drawing.
2. To make round art paper, place a plate or a bowl on a regular sheet of paper and trace around the edge. Then cut the circle out with scissors. Make some circles from colored paper and paper with different textures or thicknesses. Great big circles can be made by tracing a mixing bowl or pizza pan. Jar lids work well for smaller circles. The left-over circles from paint dispensers make even tinier circles.
   Note: Save the cut away scraps in a box for other art projects.
3. When creating art in the round, there is no flat bottom edge of the paper to be the ground and no flat top edge to be the sky. This is a very different way to draw or paint. Young artists must first think about what kind of designs fit better in a circle than a square. Many ideas for round designs are all around everywhere, such as -
   - big truck tires
   - kaleidoscope designs
   - pools of water with colorful goldfish
   - outer space or an imaginary planet
   - round flowers
   - snowflakes
   - a world where the outside of the circle is the ground and the middle the sky
4. Draw or paint a round circle picture with crayons, pencils, chalk, marking pens, or any kind of paint. Make the circle art realistic or abstract. Round pictures on round paper can just go 'round and 'round!

Da Vinci 1452-1519

*Leonardo da Vinci's (DUH-**VIN**-CHEE) sketchbook is filled with drawings and inventions with many of his notes written backwards so the words must be read with a mirror*

Drawing Things Apart

MATERIALS
- something to take apart
- tools and an adult helper
- pencil, eraser and pens
- sketchbook or white drawing paper

PROCESS
1. There are many things that can be drawn from the inside out. Some things are easy to take apart. For other things, adult's help will be needed for using tools safely and working safely.
2. Here are a few suggestions of the objects that could be taken apart:

a broken cassette tape	a ball point pen
a grapefruit, orange or artichoke cut in half	a flashlight
a computer disk that no longer works	a stapler
a chicken wing from last night's dinner	a broken video tape
an old squirt gun	a flower bud sliced in half
an old, broken appliance	an old, broken watch

3. Draw the chosen object from the outside first, as it appears everyday, before it is taken apart. Include all the details that can be seen in the drawing:

   screws   lettering   switches   textures   threads   edges

4. Next, take the object apart. Ask for adult help if needed to use tools, or if the object has dangerous parts inside.
5. Now draw the inside of the object. If there are parts that lift out, draw them too. Find out the names of the parts and label the drawing with neatly lettered words and tiny arrows just like da Vinci would do if he took something apart and then drew pictures of it. Draw until the picture seems to have all its details and seems complete.

Leonardo da Vinci

Leonardo da Vinci was a painter, a sculptor, an architect, an engineer, a town planner, an inventor, a scientist, a writer, and a musician. He was one of the greatest geniuses the world has ever known.

Da Vinci lived in Italy about 500 years ago during a famous period of art and learning called the Renaissance, a time of new ideas and inventions. Leonardo wanted to learn everything he could about the world. He asked questions about everything. He took things apart and drew pictures of every little detail he found inside. He was one of the first scientists to cut open dead animals and humans so that he could study the muscles, bones, and organs inside. Da Vinci's drawings of the human body were so good that doctors used his pictures in medical books for hundreds of years.

Young artists can draw the insides of things too. Choose an object that can be taken apart easily, and draw it from the outside and the inside. Ask permission before taking something apart, because it may not go back together again!

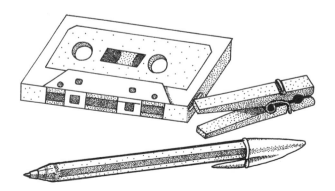

Da Vinci 1452-1519

*Da Vinci (DUH-**VIN**-CHEE) filled notebooks with his drawings of ideas and inventions that would change the world and make life easier or better in some way. He even imagined a flying machine over 500 years ago.*

Da Vinci Invention

MATERIALS

For the design —
- drawing paper or notebook of plain paper
- pencil

For the invention —
- scissors
- large paper to cover boxes
- tempera paints in containers
- paintbrushes
- tape, glue, stapler
- paper, variety of sizes
- boxes, variety of sizes
- other supplies and materials

PROCESS

1. Sit down and think of new ideas and inventions. Think and think. Think of things that can be built and would be a new way to do something. Usually an invention makes work easier or improves the world in some way. For example, a new invention might be a dog food bowl that would automatically drop just the right amount of dog food from a chute into a bowl at the dog's dinner time. This idea for an invention has never been built, but it might be a good idea.

2. What other ideas are possible? Draw as many ideas as possible on the drawing paper or in the notebook. Not all of these will be built. Just draw and draw, filling the paper with as many ideas as can be thought of.

3. Now look at the drawings of ideas and inventions. Choose one that might be fun or interesting to build.

4. Collect materials from junk, collectibles and recyclables that will be suitable for the invention. Paint, paper, boxes, and other materials will come in handy. This invention may not really work, but the experience of building will be interesting and creative.

5. Build the invention. It is okay to change the design while building. Use tape, glue, staplers, boxes, or whatever supplies are on hand. Paint the invention if desired.

6. When the invention is built, tell everyone all about the great new invention and how it will make life better or more fun. Think up a name for the invention, too.

Jordan Drost, age 11,
Ladder Chair

Da Vinci Continued

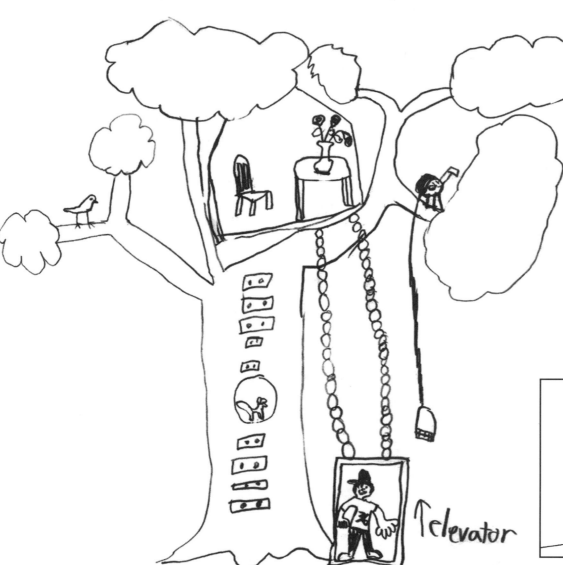

Leonardo da Vinci

Leonardo da Vinci was not only one of the greatest artists of all time, he was a great scientist and inventor too. Da Vinci was called a Renaissance man, meaning that he was devoted to thinking up new ideas both in art and in science. He has left notebooks filled with his drawings of ideas and inventions that would change the world and make life easier or better in some way. Some of the ideas were actually built as inventions, but others remained ideas on paper. Da Vinci's sketchbooks filled with drawings and inventions have notes written backwards so the words must be read with a mirror.

Young artists think up inventions and then build one, just like Leonardo da Vinci. Just like Da Vinci, the invention may or may not actually work, but the process will be an experience in design and three dimensional sculpture.

Jackie Lemon, age 9,
Tree House Elevator Invention

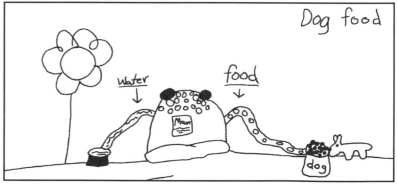

Madeline Vander Pol, age 8,
Dog Feeder Invention

Dürer 1471-1528

Albrecht Dürer

The great German artist, Albrecht Dürer, grew up in the city of Nuremberg about 500 years ago. His father was a goldsmith, and Dürer spent much of his childhood working in his father's shop, learning to make jewelry, engrave metal ornaments, and build fine sculptures. He especially liked to make woodprints.

Dürer settled in his home city of Nuremburg and opened his own studio. He painted pictures and made hundreds of beautiful prints. A set of religious prints Dürer created early in his career was sold all over Europe and brought the handsome young artist fame and recognition. He was one of the most famous artists of the Renaissance period, a time when new ideas and inventions were welcomed and encouraged. He was fascinated by detail in all aspects of his work – in oil painting, portrait drawing, watercolors, and woodcuts.

Young artists experience making a woodblock print by hammering designs into a block of wood, then covering the wood with paint, and finally making a print of the design.

Dürer (DER) was fascinated by detail in all aspects of his work – in oil painting, portrait drawing, watercolors, and woodcuts. Of all the forms of printmaking, woodcuts are the most ancient.

Wood Block Print

MATERIALS

- piece or block of soft wood, such as - pine, a weathered board, or balsa wood
- hammer
- soft cloth
- brayer or homemade roller
- water soluble printmaking ink or thick tempera paint
- tray or plate to roll ink on
- paper to print on
- collection of metal pieces to make impressions in wood, such as -

screwdriver	nuts and bolts	old jewelry pieces
nails	screws	washers

PROCESS

1. Place a small metal object on the wood and pound it with the hammer until it leaves an impression in the wood's surface. If using soft wood like pine or balsa, only a little pounding will be necessary. Note: Adult supervision is necessary with the hammering of the metal pieces. If metal pieces are especially small or thin, covering them with a cloth before hammering will help protect fingers and keep the metal pieces in place without holding them.

2. Make other hammered impressions into the wood block with different objects creating an abstract design.
   Note: Some objects, like metal bolts and washers, will make impressions with interesting shapes. Nails will make round dots. Other tools, like the tip of a flat screwdriver, make short lines. By moving the screwdriver just a bit and tapping it again, a long line can be drawn in the wood.

3. To make a print, roll a thin layer of ink or paint on the design block. Try to keep the ink on the flat surface of the wood and not get too much into the lines and impressions.

4. Next place a sheet of paper on top of the inked wood and rub hard with fingers. Try not to let the paper wiggle or the print will be wiggly too. Pull up a corner of the paper to peek at the wood print design. When ready, pull off the paper to see the finished print.

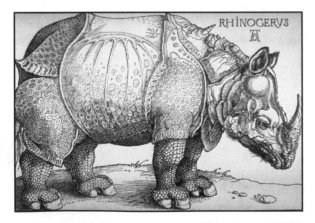

Dürer, Rhinoscerous, 1500

Raphael 1483-1520

Raphael (RAH-FY-**EL**) was considered a child prodigy, which means, even as a child he painted like an accomplished adult.

Mother and Baby

MATERIALS
- practice notebook or sketch pad
- pencil
- large sheet of paper
- thin paint wash of light brown or gray (tempera paint thinned with water)
- scissors
- crayons
- wide soft, paintbrush

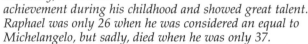

Geneva Faulkner, age 8, Mother, Baby, & Angels

PROCESS

To practice and experiment –

1. Begin by drawing some large ovals with the pencil on the sketch pad.
2. Then try to create different facial expressions on the ovals. Sometimes it helps to make a faint cross on the oval to guide where the eyes, nose, and mouth will go.
3. Add hair, hats, and other ideas to the ovals, all in a quick, sketchy manner.

To begin –

1. Cut the paper into a circle, or cut away the top of the paper in an arched shape like the walls on which Raphael painted.
2. Think of a mother and a baby and what they look like. Next, draw two ovals with the pencil, one for the mother, and a smaller one for the baby. The ovals can be close together if the mother will be holding the child.
3. Sketch other parts of the drawing, such as the hair and clothing of the mother and baby. Spend extra time on the facial features and expression of the mother and baby. Eyebrows will help define the expression more than any other facial feature.
4. Draw some angels here and there near the border too, if desired.
5. With crayons, begin to color and fill in the drawing paying special attention to the facial features and facial expressions. Color until the drawing is complete.
6. With a wide, soft brush, wash over the crayon drawing with a light brown or gray tempera paint thinned with water to fill in the remaining uncolored white paper and give the drawing an aged, antique look.

Rafaello Sanzio, known as Raphael

Raphael was a magnificent Italian painter who painted at the same time as Leonardo da Vinci and Michelangelo and is one of the three great masters of the Renaissance. Raphael grew up as the son of a painter and was surrounded with art, creativity, and artistic achievement during his childhood and showed great talent. Raphael was only 26 when he was considered an equal to Michelangelo, but sadly, died when he was only 37.

Raphael liked to paint stories from the Bible. He painted huge, detailed murals on the walls of a church that would show an entire story and all its happenings. He is best known and loved for his paintings showing a mother, her child with angels tucked in around the edges, often painting within the shape of an archway or circle to frame his picture. But most important, Raphael was known for the new attention he devoted to facial expression.

The young artist explores drawing a mother and child with crayons or colored pencils, and concentrating on facial expressions.

Raphael, Madonna della Sectia, 1510

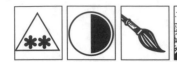

Michelangelo 1475-1564

Michelangelo Buonarroti

Florentine sculptor, painter, poet and architect Michelangelo was born at Caprese, Italy where his father was a Florentine official. Michelangelo was trained in Florence in the style of a fresco painter and then studied at the Medici School where he became a sculptor. He was friends with many interesting people at the Medici School including philosophers, artists, poets, and writers. As Michelangelo traveled and worked as an artist, he became highly well-known and was asked by Pope Julius II to paint the ceiling of the Sistine Chapel in the Vatican with frescoes, a technique he knew well. However, the job was an enormous undertaking that took over four years of working single-handed while lying on his back. To those who knew him, Michelangelo was called "The Divine Michelangelo".

The art technique Michelangelo used was called "fresco", or painting on wet plaster walls and ceilings. When the plaster is damp, the paint is absorbed into the plaster and gives a longer lasting finished work. Young artists experience fresco painting with simple watercolors or tempera paints and an inexpensive bag of plaster of Paris to make a plaque to hang on the wall.

*Michelangelo (**MY-KUL-AN-JEH-LO**) used an art technique called "fresco", which means painting on fresh, wet plaster on a wall or ceiling.*

Fresco Plaque

MATERIALS

- material for a mold, such as, a cardboard box, a pie tin, or a paper plate
- plaster of Paris
- water, container
- stick or paint stirrer
- paper clip or piece of yarn
- paintbrush
- watercolor paints or tempera paints

PROCESS

1. Mix plaster of Paris according to directions on the package in a container.
2. Pour the thick, white mixture into any chosen mold.
3. Smooth the plaster with a stick.
4. Insert a hanging device such as a paper clip or a loop of yarn while the plaster is still liquid. (See illustration.)
5. Let the plaster set up briefly so that it is damp but not too wet.
6. Gently remove the mold from around the plaster. Work carefully so the plaque does not break. Turn the plaque over to the flat side that was in the bottom of the pan. Paint on the wet plaster. As long as the plaster is damp, the paint will absorb and the fresco technique will work well.
7. Let the plaster dry overnight on the work table.
8. Hang the fresco on a wall or give it a place of honor in a bookshelf.

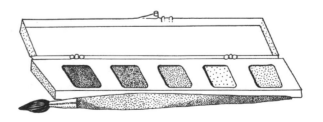

Michelangelo 1475-1564

One of Michelangelo's (MY-KUL-AN-JEH-LO) most famous and best loved works is his painting on the ceiling of the Sistine Chapel which he painted entirely while lying on his back.

Lie-Down Painting

MATERIALS
- large sheet of butcher or poster paper
- masking tape
- large school table (at child height) or coffee table
- tempera paints and brushes in sturdy cans or jars
- floor under table covered with newspaper
- artist in old clothes, bandanna over hair optional
- rags, paper towels, or sponges for clean up

PROCESS
1. Tape a large sheet of butcher paper or poster paper to the underside of a table, such as a child's school table or a household coffee table. The artist should be able to lie on his or her back under the table and comfortably reach the paper taped to the table with a paintbrush.
2. Cover the work area under the table with newspaper.
3. Assemble paints in jars or cans. Have brushes ready, one in each color of paint.
4. Lie down under the table. Relax and be comfortable. Paints should be within easy reach.
5. Begin painting on the "ceiling" of the table. Paint any subject or design desired. Note: Don't be surprised about drips and drops of paint falling from the "ceiling".
6. Leave the painting on the underside of the table to dry for several hours.
7. Remove the dry painting and display the "ceiling painting" on the ceiling of any room with additional tape.

Michelangelo Buonarroti
Italian painter and sculptor, Michelangelo, was the greatest Renaissance artist of all time. His greatest love was the study of the human body, both in painting and in sculpture. He concentrated on observing the human body and was often allowed into hospitals to study bodies of those who had died. Some say that had Michelangelo been left to himself to sculpt instead of paint, he would have become a sculptor because no other form of art so beautifully expressed the richness of the human body.

One of Michelangelo's best known and loved works is his painting on the ceiling of the Sistine Chapel. Michelangelo painted the ceiling entirely while lying on his back. To do this, he had to build a tall, strong scaffold with wooden planks (like a big ladder with a floor to stand on) so that he could climb the scaffold and be close enough to the ceiling to paint it. He assembled his paints and brushes, and lay down on his back to paint, which took four years to complete the entire ceiling!

Young artists experience the challenge of painting like Michelangelo by taping a large sheet of paper to the underside of a table and lying down to paint a scene.

*Michelangelo, Father God,
from the Sistine Chapel ceiling, 1512*

El Greco 1541-1614

Domenikos Theotokopoulos, known as El Greco

El Greco was born on the Greek island of Crete, but settled in Spain where he became a great painter, sculptor, and architect. He was known as El Greco, which means "the Greek", but his real name was Domenikos Theotocopoulos. Not much is known of his childhood. He probably showed talent as an artist by painting religious icon pictures for his local church. He left Crete as a young man to study art in the Italian city of Venice.

El Greco did not become popular until he moved to Spain in 1577 and began painting religious scenes for the cathedral in Toledo. The tall, solemn figures in El Greco's paintings appear to be stretched out — their legs, necks, arms and faces are longer and thinner than real people have. El Greco's paintings seem like pictures of another world. He often used cool blue colors to express intense religious emotions and was one of the first great artists who thought showing feelings in his artwork was more important than showing reality.

Young artists experience drawing stretched out people using photographs cut from old magazines.

The tall, solemn figures in El Greco's (EL GREH-KO) paintings appear to be stretched out.

Drawing Tall Figures

MATERIALS
- photographs of people cut from old magazines
- scrap paper
- tracing paper or thin paper
- scissors
- glue stick
- pencil and eraser

PROCESS
1. The paintings of El Greco are filled with long, tall people. The figures are stretched out much taller than real people. Draw really tall people by tracing a cut-apart photograph of a person from an old magazine. Start by cutting a picture of a person out of a magazine. Find a photo that shows the whole figure from the feet to the top of the head.
2. Cut across the photo several times. Cut at the ankles, knees, hips, waist, chest and neck. This divides the photo-person into sections. Glue these sections on scrap paper, spreading the pieces out so the person gets very tall and stretched out.
3. Put a sheet of tracing paper over the sliced photo. Trace around the figure. Follow the edges of the photo and use imagination to connect the gaps between the slices.
4. Remove the sliced photo and finish the long, tall person drawing until it seems complete.
5. Tracing over photos can be good drawing practice, especially when photos are traced and changed to fit one's own imagination.

VARIATIONS
- Use this technique to draw large, wide people too.
- Clone or mix figures together with parts from several animals and people. How about a person's body with a hawk's head?

Rubens 1577-1640

*Rubens (**ROO**-BENZ) was a master by the time he was 21. He lived a happy life with his family, and created many drawings of his children with chalk on brown paper.*

Chalk Light Face

MATERIALS
- pastel chalks in black, red-brown and white colors
- brown paper grocery bags
- brown and tan construction paper
- scissors

PROCESS
1. Cut several grocery bags apart to make sheets of brown drawing paper, or select construction paper in brown and tan colors.
2. Ask a friend or someone in the family to sit still for a few minutes to be a model. With the white chalk, very lightly sketch the outline shape of the model's head on the brown paper. Work very big. Make light marks where the eyes, nose and mouth will go.
3. Next work slowly with black chalk over the white lines, carefully drawing the model's face. Look up at the model often, then back down to the drawing. The drawing may not end up looking like the model, but it will be an interesting way to experience what Rubens might have felt or seen.
4. When finished with the black lines, hold a piece of red-brown chalk on its side and rub it gently over the parts of the drawing that are dark, the shadows and perhaps the hair. Rub black chalk onto the very darkest shadow places.
5. Finally, hold the white chalk on its side and make highlights on the lightest areas of the drawing, usually the forehead, the cheeks and a glitter in the eyes. The white chalk will show up nicely on the brown paper and look like light shining on the drawing.

Peter Paul Rubens

The Flemish painter Peter Paul Rubens was the most famous northern European artist of his day. Rubens grew up in Antwerp, Holland, and was considered a master painter by the time he was 21. In 1600, he left home to study art in Italy and Spain, and became well known for creating altar pieces and religious paintings in Venice and Rome. After nearly 10 years in Italy, he returned to settle in Antwerp.

Rubens was a religious man, full of energy and love for his work. He set up a studio, like those of the early Renaissance, with dozens of artists working under his direction in one room. Rubens sketched pictures and directed the artwork for many huge paintings, commissioned by his royal patrons, Archduke Ferdinand and Archduchess Isabella of Spain. Rubens was also a diplomat, and often had to interrupt his artwork to negotiate peace treaties in battles between Spain and England.

Rubens had a happy family life, and made many pictures of his children. His sketches were done with black, red-brown and white chalk on brown paper. Young artists sketch family and friends the same way, using the insides of brown grocery bags for paper.

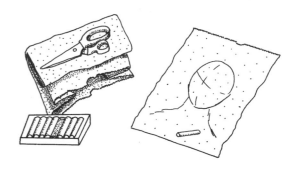

Rembrandt 1606-1669

Rembrandt Harmensz van Rijn

Rembrandt was born in Holland in 1606. His full name was Rembrandt Harmensz van Rijn. There are only a few people in history who are so famous that they're known by their first names and Rembrandt is one of them! He was an important artist when he was alive, and his fame has grown greater through the years. The paintings, drawings and prints he created are priceless.

Rembrandt liked to practice by making drawings of himself. He would look in a mirror and draw what he saw. He especially enjoyed making faces at himself and drawing his wild expressions, such as, shocked, fearful, angry, or happy.

Young artists explore drawing faces and expressions the same way — with a sketch-pad, pencil, mirror, and a face to make funny faces!

*There are only a few people in history who are so famous that they're known by their first names and Rembrandt (**RHEM**-BRANT) is one of them.*

Making Faces!

MATERIALS
- sketchpad or drawing paper
- pencil
- mirror

PROCESS
1. Stand in front of the bathroom mirror with a sketchpad and pencil, or find a small mirror that can be propped up on the table and sit in front of it.
2. Look at your face in the mirror. Notice eyes, eyebrows, mouth. Start by drawing your face without any special expression, just gazing calmly ahead. Look closely at your reflection and try to draw what you actually see in the mirror.
3. Next, try drawing an expression on a new sheet of paper! Look into the mirror as you make a really angry face, noticing eyes, eyebrows, and mouth. How are they different from the first calm expression you drew? Draw your angry face.
   (It might feel funny making faces at yourself, but remember that you're an artist just like Rembrandt, and this is a great way to practice!)
4. Draw lots of different expressions. Write the date on each drawing and save them in a notebook. Here are some expressions to draw by watching your face in a mirror:

angry	surprised	fear	sad
joyful	worried	disgusted	frustrated
confused	tired	shy	frightened

mad   sad   scared   sneaky   nervous

Rembrandt, Night Watch, 1642

Jesse Vander Hoek, age 8, Facial Expressions

Rembrandt 1606-1669

*Photography had not been invented in Rembrandt's (**RHEM**-BRANT) time, so hiring him as an artist was the only way to get a "picture portrait" taken.*

Shadowy Faces

MATERIALS
- a friend who will model
- drawing paper
- pencil
- a dark room
- a small lamp or spotlight

PROCESS
1. Have a friend sit in a chair right next to a lamp or spotlight. Turn the room lights down low, and place the lamp so that a bright light shines on one side of the friend's face.
2. Sketch the friend's face as he or she sits still. Draw the edges of the chin and neck, the hair and lips. Draw the eyes and nose. Look carefully and try to draw what is seen. Remember to draw the eyebrows.
3. The shadows on the friend's face will be the next thing to draw. Look carefully to see how shadows fall around the nose, chin, hair and forehead. Lightly sketch the shapes of the shadows, then hold a pencil on its side to shade them in.
4. Trade places, and sit still while the friend has a turn to draw.

VARIATIONS
Suggestions of models who might hold still while their portraits are drawn:
- mom sitting and reading a book
- grandpa relaxing in a chair and looking out the window
- dad snoozing in his easy chair
- baby sister asleep in her crib

Rembrandt Harmensz van Rijn

Rembrandt was famous for painting portraits. He made pictures of himself and of everyone in his family. People paid him money to paint their pictures. Photography had not been invented in Rembrandt's time, so hiring an artist was the only way to get your "picture taken." Rembrandt liked to use strong lighting to add interest to a face. He would show half of a person's face with bright sunlight falling on it, and the other half in deep shadow. Young artists draw pictures of their friends with bright light and dark shadow, just like Rembrandt.

Kim Solga, student art, Shadow Face

Linnaeus 1707-1778

Carl Linnaeus

Carl Linnaeus was one of the world's most famous botanists, a scientist who studied plants. He grew up in southern Sweden and was the son of a church pastor. Linnaeus's father kept a large garden filled with plants he enjoyed collecting. As a boy, Linnaeus loved to study the different kinds of plants that grew there. He went on to medical school and became a doctor and a scientist of great fame.

Many scientists use art in their work. Botanists, who study plants, often draw and paint beautiful pictures of flowers, leaves, stems and roots in fine detail. Linnaeus would sketch the details of the tiny parts of different flowers, and then would hire artists to illustrate his books and scientific papers.

Young artists experience being a botanical illustrator by taking a walk, picking a flower, and then drawing it in careful detail, inside and out.

Linnaeus, c. 1760, Sunflowers

When Carl Linnaeus (LIHN-AY-IS) was a child, he loved to study the plants in his father's garden.

Botanical Illustrations

MATERIALS
- choice of a flower or weed-blossom from a garden (or a flower shop)
- white drawing paper
- pencil and eraser
- colored pencils or crayons
- magnifying glass

PROCESS
1. Go for a walk through the neighborhood. Find a flower for the botanical illustration with a simple blossom like a daisy or a blossom from a weed. The flower should have a stem and leaves. It might be possible to pull up a tiny flower with its roots. Ask permission to take any flower growing in a garden or park. Then return to the art table to begin a botanical illustration.
2. Place the flower on the table beside the drawing paper and sketch a picture of its exact shape and size. Put in as many details as possible, such as leaves, roots, stems, flower buds and petals. Make the drawing life size, so if the real flower were placed on top of the sketch, it would fit exactly.
3. On the same drawing paper, but next to this main drawing, draw close-up views of different parts of the flower. Draw the center of the blossom, using a magnifying glass to see the tiny parts like stamen and sepals. Draw a leaf flattened out with all the veins and edges. If one is available to study, draw a flower bud before it blooms.
4. For additional help, use an encyclopedia or library book about flowers to find the names of the different parts of the flower. Add these names to the drawing with neat lettering and little arrows showing which parts they go with.
5. Color the drawing to match the natural colors of the plant with crayons or colored pencils.

Gainsborough 1727-1788

*Gainsborough (**GAYNZ**-BER-O) liked to paint fancy, imaginary landscapes.*

Portrait on Landscape

MATERIALS

For the landscape painting -
- large drawing paper
- tempera paints, mixed medium/thin
- paintbrushes
- jar of clear water for rinsing
- newspaper covered work area

For the portrait drawings -
- drawing paper
- marking pens
- scissors
- glue

PROCESS

1. Paint an imaginary landscape with the paints on the large drawing sheet. Some ideas to include might be -

trees	clouds	rivers	rocks	roads
paths	flowers	waterfall	fields	mountains

2. Allow the painting to dry.
3. While the painting dries, draw the portrait of one or two people who will fit into the imaginary landscape. Draw their full bodies sitting or standing and holding still in their pose (not running or fishing or dancing).
4. Cut out the portraits and spread the backs with a little glue. Press the portraits into the landscape. Now the people are part of the imaginary landscape. Dry.

VARIATIONS

- Draw any imaginary landscape or background scene imaginable, such as -

  outer space   under the sea   outdoor winter scene
  in Santa's workshop   at the circus or zoo   in a classroom

  Then draw and cut-out appropriate character portraits of people, animals, aliens, fish, elves, and so on and glue them into the appropriate scene.

Thomas Gainsborough

Thomas Gainsborough was an English painter of landscapes and portraits. He was the leading portrait painter in England throughout his lifetime. It seemed that everyone in England wanted to have their portraits painted by Gainsborough. Gainsborough preferred to paint what might be called fancy landscapes, that is, landscapes that are more ideal and imaginary than real. He would often include the portraits of people as part of the fancy landscape.

To explore Gainsborough's style of fancy landscapes mixed with portraits, young artists paint an imaginary landscape and then glue cut-out portraits into the scenery.

Nici Smith, age 11, Desert Watercolor
Tatiana Huaracha, age 8, Picnic People

Blake 1757-1827

William Blake

William Blake was a painter, a printmaker, and a poet. He grew up in the great British city of London, attending school and working in his father's store. When he was 14, his father apprenticed him to an engraver, where Blake learned the skills of drawing and making prints.

Blake is best known for his gentle and mystical illustrations of religious scenes. One of his first works was a book he called "Songs of Innocence". Blake made prints of his own poems illustrated with beautiful drawings. His wife and partner, Catherine, printed the pictures, then colored them by hand and bound the pages into books. Young artists explore making prints with black tempera paint or ink and hand color them when they are dry.

"To see a World in a Grain of Sand, And a Heaven in a Wild Flower, Hold Infinity in the palm of your hand, And Eternity in an hour." – Blake (BLAYK)

Hand Colored Prints

MATERIALS
- black tempera paint or water soluble printmaking ink
- white drawing paper
- cookie sheet
- colored pencils or markers
- brayer (art roller with a handle)
- tools to draw in the wet paint, such as -
    pencil, stick, toothpick, cotton swab, stiff paintbrush, wad of tissue, finger

PROCESS
1. Squeeze some black paint or washable printer's ink onto a flat cookie sheet.
2. Roll the brayer through the paint to smooth it into a thin, even layer.
3. Next, scratch a picture or design into the paint with any chosen drawing tools. Work quickly so the black paint does not dry. (Like finger-painting!) Hint: A pencil or toothpick will scratch fine lines. Wide sticks will scrape away wide areas of paint. A stiff paintbrush, tissues, or even fingers will pat or brush areas of texture. Note: The print is always a reversal of whatever is drawn.
4. For this next step, wash and dry hands so fingers are clean. Carefully place a sheet of white drawing paper over the black paint drawing. Try not to wiggle the paper. Rub it gently with the flat of the hand. Then lift up and peel away the paper. The design will be transferred onto the paper. Set this print aside to dry.
5. Roll more black paint onto the cookie sheet, make more designs, and make another print. Experiment with ideas such as -
    - make lines and textures with different types of tools
    - rub and press the paper harder when taking the print
    - rub and press the paper more gently when taking the print
    - use colors of ink or paint other than black
6. Continue experimenting and making as many prints as desired.
7. Later, when the black paint or ink on the prints is completely dry, color-in the lighter areas of the prints with colored pencils or colored marking pens.

Constable 1776-1837

*When asked what inspired him most, John Constable (**CON**-STUH-BUL) said, "The sound of water escaping from mill dams, willows, old rotten planks, slimy posts and brickwork, I love such things. These scenes made me a painter."*

Cloudscape

MATERIALS

- pencil and eraser
- white drawing paper or watercolor paper
- flat board or tabletop and masking tape
- watercolor paints and water
- paintbrushes in a variety of small and large sizes
- scrap paper for testing paint colors
- facial tissues

PROCESS

1. Sketch an outdoor scene with very light pencil lines on white paper. Draw from imagination, sketch a picture from a magazine, or go outside and draw an actual outdoor scene near home or school.
2. Tape the paper onto a board or tabletop using long strips of masking tape so the paper is completely taped down on all four sides.
3. To make light sky-blue color with watercolors, simply mix dark blue paint with water in the cover of the watercolor box or in a dish. Mix up lots of blue paint, more than may seem necessary to paint the sky in the drawing. Test the paint mixture on scrap paper until a preferred color is reached.
4. Now quickly paint the entire sky in the drawing, covering the paper with wet, blue paint. Work very fast with two paintbrushes, a big one to cover the open areas, and a smaller one to paint all around the hills, trees and other features in the sketch. Then right away, before the watercolor has a chance to dry or even soak in to the white paper, use facial tissues to pat out several puffy white clouds. Dab the tissue down onto the sky, soaking up the blue paint and showing the white paper beneath. The tissue leaves a blurry edge between blue and white, just like real clouds might look in the sky.
5. Let the sky and clouds dry completely before finishing the painting. Paint the rest of the outdoor scene on the dry cloudscape with greens, reds, blues and any other favorite colors. Let this part of the painting dry completely before peeling away the masking tape.
6. Finally, lift the cloudscape painting off the board. A clean frame will be left from the masking tape.

John Constable

John Constable started painting when he was a young boy in school and growing up in the English countryside. He was the son of a wealthy businessman. Constable loved to go hiking and take his sketchbooks and watercolors along. He was encouraged to become a painter both by his family and by neighbors who were amateur painters. Constable became one of the best known landscape artists of his time, painting the places he knew best—the fields, hills and farms near his home, and the nearby seaside. When asked what inspired him most, he answered, "The sound of water escaping from mill dams, willows, old rotten planks, slimy posts and brickwork. I love such things. These scenes made me a painter."

When the clouds are the main interest of the painting, it is called a cloudscape. Young artists explore painting a cloudscape in the style of Constable, with clear blue skies and sparkling white clouds!

Tim Dettman, age 12,
Palm Tree with Cloud Sky

Hokusai 1760-1849

Katsushika Hokusai

The Japanese artist, Hokusai, was born over 200 years ago. He began illustrating when he was very young and painted more than 30,000 paintings during his life. Hokusai lived his 89 years as an illustrator in Japan. But work was scarce and Hokusai had to move from town to town to find enough work to live.

During his lifetime he called himself by more than 30 names. The last name he gave himself was "An Old Man Crazy for Art".

Hokusai was well known for sketching and painting ordinary daily scenes from his life and for making woodblock prints, which he later painted with watercolors or inks. He designed and illustrated lovely small greeting cards called surimono. Surimono were intended to be given as gifts from one friend or family member to another, especially as a greeting for a happy new year or other holiday wish. A poet would write the special verse or saying on the paper, and an illustrator like Hokusai would interpret the poem through drawings. Young artists do both: be the poet and be the artist.

During his lifetime Hokusai (HO-KOO-SY) called himself by more than 30 names. The last name he gave himself was "An Old Man Crazy for Art".

Surimono Greeting

MATERIALS

For the surimono:
- white paper
- fine point markers, crayons, or colored pencils
- patterned wallpaper scraps
- scissors
- pen to write poem or words

For the name tile (artist's signature):
- large square eraser
- scratching tool such as a heavy un-bent paperclip
- red ink pad (for a homemade pad, drop paint or food coloring on a paper towel)

PROCESS

1. Read some greeting cards out loud to get some ideas about nice greetings. Then make up a greeting and write it on the white piece of paper. The greeting should be easy to illustrate. For example, a greeting might say: May your day be filled with sunshine. Or, to rhyme a greeting card, one might say: I love you in the morning, I love you in the night. I love when you're wrong, and even when you're right.

   Note: If the artist is too young to write, an adult can take dictation and write it on the card for the young artist.

2. When the greeting has been written on the paper, illustrate the greeting with a "surimono" (a drawing and decoration) for the greeting card. The greeting and illustration may be on the front of the paper, folded inside the paper, or any other card design of choice. Add wallpaper scraps as colorful borders on the card to look like fancy Japanese papers.

3. To "sign" the greeting card, scratch a design into a square eraser with a paperclip that has been straightened or use some other small tool. The design could be scratched to look like Japanese letters, one's own initials, or any design at all.

4. Press the scratched design into the red ink pad. Then press the inked eraser on the greeting card in the lower right corner. Now the card is signed in the same fashion Hokusai used over 200 years ago when he signed his name.

5. Give the surimono to someone special. It is a one-of-a-kind work of art.

Audubon 1785-1851

*John James Audubon (**AH**-DUH-BAHN) painted more than 400 watercolors of wild birds in their natural settings.*

Nature Notebook

MATERIALS
- spiral bound sketchpad, several sheets of white drawing paper folded and stapled to make a small sketchbook, or paper in a 3-ring binder
- wildlife books and magazines
- pencils, colored pencils, crayons, watercolors, etc.

PROCESS
1. Draw a realistic picture of a wild animal. Look at a photo of the animal while drawing. Include all the details possible.
2. Include a realistic background in the drawing showing where the animal lives.Color the drawing with colored pencils, crayons, or paints.
3. Along the side of the drawing, write things about the animal telling its common and scientific name, where it lives, what it likes to eat, and any other facts discovered.
4. Make small sketches along the side of the drawing to show details of the animal, such as what its footprints look like in the mud or snow, or draw a close up of its ear, beak or paw.
5. Collect sketches of many different animals in the Nature Notebook.

John James Audubon
John James Audubon is one of the most famous painters of birds in the world. Audubon was born more than 200 years ago on the Caribbean island of Santo Domingo. His father was a sea captain. Audubon and his family later moved to France where he grew up. In 1802, his father sent him to live in the new country called the United States.

Audubon loved America, especially the wildlife and the beautiful birds. He made it his life's work to paint a picture of every species of bird in America, traveling from Florida to Texas to northern Canada to observe wild birds and paint their pictures. He painted 435 watercolors of birds.

Young artists collect drawings and facts about wild birds and animals from their own neighborhoods, family travels, or from magazines and books to save in an individually created a Nature Notebook, similar to the way Audubon kept track of his wildlife notes.

Chad Noward, age 7,
Squirrel Sketch

Courbet 1819-1877

Gustave Courbet

Gustave Courbet was the son of a rich farming family in France. He was sent to Paris in 1841 to become a lawyer, but Courbet decided to study painting instead. By 1844 he began showing his paintings at important shows and galleries. Courbet was a Realist which means he believed that paintings should show things as they really are, not how they are felt or imagined. Courbet often chose to paint poor people hard at work rather than wealthy patrons relaxing in their palaces. He enjoyed life and filled his paintings with rich colors, beautiful landscapes, and handsome people.

Earlier artists had learned how to create texture in their pictures with stiff brushes and thick gobs of paint, but Courbet was probably the first artist to use a palette knife. Courbet used a thin knife with a dull blade that bent easily to spread paint thin like buttering toast, scratch in lines and gouges into wet paint, and smear thick ridges. Young artists explore learning to paint with a palette knife and thick paint in the style of Courbet.

Courbet (COR-BAY) was the first artist to use a palette knife to create texture in painting, a technique like spreading peanut butter on a slice of bread.

Palette Knife Painting

MATERIALS
- acrylic paints squeezed from tubes, or tempera paint thickened with wallpaper paste
- inexpensive metal or plastic palette knife or a popsicle stick
- paper board, such as matte board, foamboard or white cardboard
- pencil

PROCESS
1. Start by experimenting with an abstract paint design. Squeeze or spoon 3 or 4 colors of paint onto a paper board. Use the palette knife or popsicle stick to spread the paint and create a design. Think of it as finger-painting with a tool instead of with fingers.
2. Use the palette knife to move the thick paint around in different ways. Spread the paint thin like buttering toast, make swirls of paint like frosting a cake, scratch lines into layers of paint, or pat the knife against wet paint to make a bumpy surface. Squish different colors of paint together to mix them and make new colors.
3. When comfortable with using the palette knife, start another picture. This time try to paint something realistic, like a small branch with leaves or a single flower blossom. Sketch the picture with a pencil first.
   Note: It might help to bring a leafy twig into the art area to look at while working.
4. Use the tip of the palette knife to paint the twig and then make the leaves. Try to do the entire picture without using a paintbrush!
5. Dry the painting overnight. Note: Thick paint takes longer to dry.

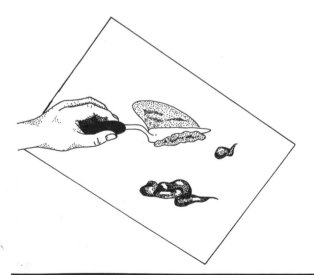

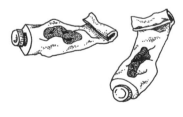

SUNNY & FREE

chapter 2

Impressionists &
Post Impressionists

Christina Critelli, age 6, Footbridge

Manet 1832-1883

Édouard Manet

Édouard Manet is considered one of the first Impressionists, but was very different from other Impressionists. He rarely painted from nature. While other painters like Monet and Courbet were out viewing the fields and ponds and painting directly from nature, Manet sat inside painting from his memory or by looking at a model. He loved the city and other Impressionists loved the country; he was well-off and refined and they were poor; he believed that art was elegant while they believed that art was casual. With all their differences, Manet was still thought of as "the shining light" of the Impressionists, an artist who incorporated light in his paintings and shined like a light to other artists.

Young artists explore Manet's Impressionist style with a melted-crayon activity that resembles the dabbled look of his paintings. And like Manet, the young artist paints a still-life indoors in the art studio instead of outside.

Manet (MAH-NAY) is thought of by everyone as "the shining light" of the Impressionists, yet he never thought of himself as an Impressionist at all.

Still-Life in Melted Crayon

MATERIALS

- warming tray or other safe heat source such as a foil lined electric frying pan
- aluminum foil
- newspaper
- old muffin tin
- old paintbrushes
- 2 sheets of drawing paper
- long cotton swabs, optional
- old broken crayons, peeled
- preheated oven set at 200° F.
- hot pads
- still life scene, such as - fruit in a bowl, pot of flowers, any group of favorite objects

PROCESS

Set up -

1. Cover the work table with newspaper. Arrange a still-life on one end of the artist's work table. Peel broken crayons and place them in the cups of the old muffin tin, separating by color.
2. Place the warming tray on the other end of the work table. Cover the tray with aluminum foil. Plug in the warming tray and allow it to begin warming.
3. With an adult helper, place the muffin tin in the preheated oven for a few minutes until the crayons melt to complete liquid. Then wear hot pads and move the muffin tin to the warming tray.

To paint -

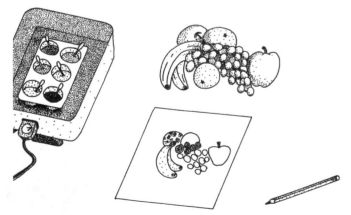

1. Dip an old paintbrush or cotton swab into the melted crayon.
2. To practice the dabbing technique, quickly dab it onto the first sheet of paper. As the crayon cools and hardens on the brush, then it will be necessary to dip back into the melted crayon. Then dab on the paper. Let the dabs join together.
3. Now spread out a fresh sheet of paper. Look at the still-life arrangement on the table. Begin dabbing melted crayon in the design of the still-life. Look at the still-life often to pick up the colors and shapes in the arrangement. Dab until the painting is complete.
4. When finished, unplug the tray and be sure the oven is off. Muffin tin and brushes can not be cleaned but can be used for all melted crayon projects.

Monet 1840-1926

Monet (MO-NAY) painted with short brush strokes and dabbles and splashes of pretty colors, catching light and reflection in his work.

Dabble in Paint

MATERIALS
- watercolor or tempera paints
- paintbrushes
- several sheets of large, heavy white paper
- an easel or a small work table
- jar of water
- rags
- postcards, posters, or prints by Monet
- outdoor area to set up a small work table or easel

PROCESS
1. Set up a table or easel outside where there are flowers or a pond to view. A sunny day will help make the painting experience more like Monet would have loved.
2. Look at prints or postcards painted by Monet. Notice his short dabbling paint strokes, like the brush is smooshed down rather than lines painted. Try dabbing and smooshing paints on a practice sheet of paper. Now brush water on the paper and practice painting in the damp area with the same dabbing and smooshing technique.
3. After practicing, remove the practice paper and set up a clean sheet.
4. Decide if the paper will be wet or dry, based on what was preferred when practicing.
5. Look at the surroundings. Begin painting using the dabbing and short stroke technique used in practice.
6. When satisfied, set the painting aside to dry.
7. Paint as many Impressionistic paintings as desired. Wouldn't Monet be impressed?

Claude Monet

Claude Monet was a French painter who is best known as the leader of the Impressionists, a group of painters who painted what they saw and felt rather than painting something exactly the way it really looked. Monet was known for painting with short brush strokes and dabbles and splashes of pretty colors, catching light and reflection in his work. Monet painted anything from simple haystacks to grand cathedrals, but he is best known for his painted impressions of lovely gardens and reflections in water of flowers and trees. One of his most famous paintings is The Footbridge (from a bridge that crossed his pond).

Monet's paintings were beautiful, but he was not always happy with them. Sometimes, he burned them when he was most dissatisfied. Thankfully, most of his beautiful paintings have survived and become the most popular and best loved works of all the Impressionists.

Young artists paint impressionistic paintings by dabbing and daubing paint on damp paper, perhaps painting flowers or water reflections like the great master, Claude Monet.

*Christina Critelli, age 6,
Footbridge*

Degas 1834-1917

Edgar Degas

Edgar Degas was a French painter, draftsman, sculptor, and graphic artist. He was the son of a rich banker. Degas studied law, but preferred painting portraits. Later, he developed his abilities in painting dancers, races, town life, and other portraits. Although he did not consider himself an Impressionist, he was grouped with them in exhibitions.

Degas studied movement of his subjects and then tried to show that movement in his art, especially the movements of dancers and racehorses.

Although Degas often worked in chalk or pastels, the young artist explores creating movement in art by drawing with crayons and then applying a tempera paint wash over the drawing.

Degas (DAY-GAH) studied movement of his subjects and then tried to show that movement in his art.

Resist in Motion

MATERIALS

- covered work area
- scissors
- heavy paper, lightweight cardboard, or tag board
- white drawing paper
- pencil
- crayons
- tempera paint wash in a jar (tempera paint thinned with water)
- wide, soft paintbrush

PROCESS

1. Draw an object on the heavy paper with the pencil, such as an animal, train, car, person, or other object that moves. Draw the object large enough and thick enough to be cut out and traced around like a stencil.
   Note: Commercially cut stencils can be used, but child-made stencils are more creative and allow the artist to explore the entire process of art.
2. Cut out the object using scissors.
3. Place the cut-out object or stencil on the white drawing paper. Trace around the stencil with a crayon.
4. Next, move the stencil slightly, perhaps a 1/2 inch or so, and trace the stencil again using a crayon of the same color or a different color.
5. Then, move the stencil slightly again, and trace. Continue moving the stencil and tracing each move, making a long line, curved or straight, with the stencils traced over and over. This repetitive tracing will make the object look like it is in motion and speeding across the paper. (See illustration.)
6. The traced shapes can be colored-in with any variety of crayon colors, or they may be left white.
7. Paint over the crayon tracings with the paint wash and a wide, soft brush.
   Note: The paint will stick to the paper but will resist the waxy crayon marks and colored areas. This is called a crayon resist.
8. Allow the resist to dry. See the object in motion across the paper?

Degas 1834-1917

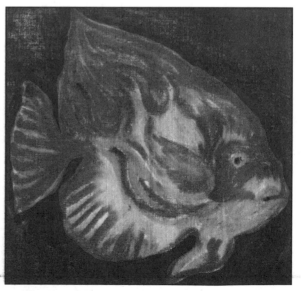

Degas (DAY-GAH) captured every moment of the work of ballet dancers, from the beginning of practice to the end of a dance performance.

Chalk on Cloth

MATERIALS
- 12" square of white cotton cloth with a rough weave, like canvas or muslin
- milk in a bowl
- colored pastel chalks
- scrap paper and an old newspaper
- piece of aluminum foil
- clothing iron and an adult to help use it

PROCESS
1. Soak the cloth in milk, then spread it out on scrap paper.
2. Draw a picture on the wet cloth with colored chalk. Work fast to complete the drawing before the cloth gets dry.
3. Flip the damp drawing over, face down, on a clean sheet of scrap paper. Set the cloth and paper on a pile of old newspapers.
4. Ask an adult to help with the next step. Before turning on the iron, cover the bottom of the iron with aluminum foil. Then have an adult turn the iron on to the "wool" setting and iron the back of the chalk drawing.
   Note: The heat on the milky cloth seals the chalk into the fabric.
5. Hang the chalk picture on the wall, put it in a frame, or use it to cover a book or a binder. Keep in mind that the chalk will wash out in the laundry, so this method won't work to decorate clothes.

Edgar Degas
Edgar Degas was one of the artists in a group of artists known as an Impressionists. These painters and sculptors lived in France about 100 years ago. Their art broke all the traditional rules of painting. For example, they used bright splashes of color, quick dashes of paintbrush and chalk, and lots of sparkling light to show scenes of everyday life.

Degas was unusual among the Impressionists. While other artists took to the countryside and gardens to find bright sun-lit scenes, Degas stayed indoors. He is best known for his pictures of dancers at the ballet and the romantic night-life of Paris. Degas used charcoal pencil and colored chalk as often as he used paint to create his artworks.

Young artists experience the magic of chalk which looks more like a painting than a drawing and is created with chalk on cloth. (The secret ingredient is milk!)

Nici Smith, age 9,
Chalk Fish

Morisot 1841-1895

Berthe Morisot

Berthe Morisot showed great talent for painting as a young girl. Even though it was unusual for women to become professional artists in the 1800's, Morisot's parents encouraged her to study art and become a professional. She became one of the original members of the Impressionists, a group of French painters who changed the nature of art in the late years of the 1800's. In those days art students visited museums and painted copies of great masterpieces for practice. One day, while Morisot was working this way at the Louvre (a famous museum in Paris), Morisot met the artist Édouard Manet. They became friends, and Manet invited Morisot to work at his studio. There she met other artists including Manet's younger brother Eugene, whom she married several years later. Women were rarely taken seriously in the art world 100 years ago, but Morisot was always admired, often selling more paintings than Monet or Renoir. Morisot created pictures with thick brush strokes, heavy globs, and bright colors.

Young artists work with thick paints, such as acrylic paints straight from the tube, or textured paints mixed from everyday tempera paints.

*Berthe Morisot (**MOR**-IH-SO) showed great talent for painting as a young girl. Even though it was unusual for women to become professional artists, Morisot's parents encouraged her to study art and become a professional.*

Texture Paints

MATERIALS
- tempera or poster paint
- jars for mixing
- texture materials, such as -

  | wallpaper paste | white flour | crushed eggshells |
  | salt | glitter | sawdust or sand |

- heavy paper or pieces of matte board, form board, or white cardboard
- paintbrushes
- popsicle sticks

PROCESS
1. Fill mixing jars with about 1/8 cup of liquid tempera paint in each. Use a different color for each cup.
2. Stir one texture material into each cup. For instance, put a spoonful of wallpaper paste or white flour into the first cup, stir, and make a thick pudding-like paint. In the second color, mix some crushed eggshells. In the third color, add sawdust or salt or sand. Each texture material will make paint with a different texture paint quality.
3. Use the texture paints to paint a picture on the heavy paper or matte board. Make a picture of a landscape, an animal, a person, or an abstract design. Explore the use of different paintbrushes and popsicle sticks to apply the texture paints.
4. Dry the painting for several hours.

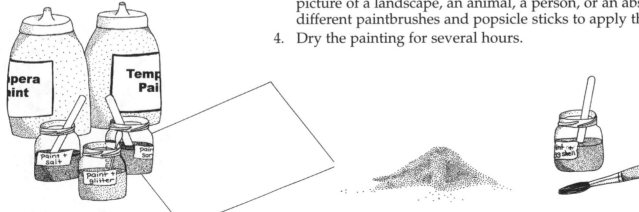

Homer 1836-1910

*Homer (**HO**-MER) liked to use bright colors in his watercolor paintings to make things appear very near and faded colors to make things look far away.*

Wilderness Watercolor

MATERIALS

- heavy white drawing paper or watercolor paper, at least 9"x 12"
- white plate or mixing areas in paintbox lid
- watercolor paint set
- jar of clear water
- paintbrush
- pencil
- black felt pen

PROCESS

1. Draw a pencil line across the upper third of the paper to represent the horizon, where land and water will meet the sky. The pencil will no longer be needed.
2. Wet the sheet of paper by holding it under a faucet or dipping it into a pan of water. Smooth the damp paper flat on a worktable. The wet paper will allow the paints to fuzz together.
3. Begin by mixing paint for the land. Mix bright green paint with water in one of the mixing areas of the paintbox cover or on a white plate. Paint the bottom third of the damp paper with bright green paint to represent the foreground or grass.
4. Next, mix paint for the trees. Mix water into the bright green color to dilute and dull the pigment. Use this paint to make some trees or bushes just above the grass.
5. Now mix paint for the mountain lake. Rinse the brush and mix a strong blue paint for the lake behind the trees and right up to the pencil line, the horizon. Leave some white stripes and spaces in the blue to look like reflections in water.
6. Now mix paint for the sky. Thin the blue paint with water to make a pale blue for the sky. Paint the entire sky with pale blue. Leave some white areas for clouds, if desired. The sky will meet the lake at the pencil line.
7. Mix a very pale green blue for mountains. Paint mountains at the horizon of the lake and into the sky.
8. Dry the painting. After the painting is completely dry, outline the lakeshore, trees, hills and mountain shapes with black felt pen. Add other details, if desired.

Winslow Homer

Winslow Homer was an American painter, journalist, and illustrator. He covered the Civil War for the magazine "Harper's Weekly". Homer was one of the first artists to create and sell watercolor paintings. Homer liked to paint the outdoors and the sea and was a master of outdoor painting scenes. He used watercolors for perspective, that is, to create the feeling that some things in a picture look far away while other things look closer. For example, bright colors make things appear to be very near. Faded colors make objects like mountains look farther away.

Young artists experiment with the technique of wet-on-wet watercolor, painting a mountain lake and the surrounding environment, experiencing Homer's style.

Aaron Avsshai, age 12, Lake and Sky

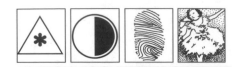

Cassatt 1845-1926

Mary Cassatt

The great Impressionist painter, Mary Cassatt, lived about 100 years ago. She grew up in America, but like many artists of her time, moved to Paris to live and work as an artist. She decided to be a professional artist when she was very young, even though her family felt it was not a proper job for a young woman. But Cassatt believed in herself, studied hard, and went on to become a famous artist.

The Impressionists were a group of artists who believed in painting pictures very different from the usual artwork of the time. They painted people in everyday scenes rather than posed portraits. Cassatt is famous for her paintings of mothers and their children. Some of her pictures are monoprints, made by painting a picture on a flat tray, then pressing paper on top of the wet paint to make a print of the image. Young artists create monoprints with an old cookie sheet, tempera paints, and paper.

When Mary Cassatt (CUH-SAHT) was very young, she decided to become a professional artist, even though her family objected because they felt it was not a proper job for a young woman.

Tempera Monoprint

MATERIALS

- tempera paint
- paintbrush
- pencil or small stick
- flat pan or cookie sheet
- white drawing paper
- paper towels

PROCESS

1. Paint a picture directly on a flat pan or cookie sheet. Use many different colors. Work fast so the paint does not get too dry.
2. Scratch lines into the painting with a pencil or small stick, similar to finger-painting.
3. Next, place a sheet of white paper on top of the wet painting and pat it gently with one hand. Try not to wiggle the paper. Lift the paper up and see the painted picture transferred onto the paper. This is a monoprint! (Mono means "one", and each painting makes one print.)
4. To make another monoprint, wipe the pan clean with paper towels and repeat steps 1 through 3.

Renoir 1841-1919

Renoir's (REN-WAH) paintings were filled with light, fresh colors. He once said, "Why shouldn't art be pretty? There are enough unpleasant things in the world."

Mixed Media Still-Life

MATERIALS
- cardboard or matte board
- white tempera paint and brush
- collect a bouquet of flowers, weeds, or leaves
- choice of any vase or container (unusual ones are fun, too), such as -
- pencil
- watercolor paints

vase	milk carton	soup can	pop bottle	jar
tennis shoe	crate or box	mug	planting pot	tea pot

PROCESS
1. Paint a piece of cardboard or matte board with a heavy coat of white tempera paint.
2. While the white paint is drying, take a walk and collect a bouquet of any chosen flowers, weeds, leaves, plants, or branches. Any selection of growies are fine, depending on the choice of the young artist.
3. Part of the fun is choosing a unique or unusual vase or container such as a shoe or a soup can. Arrange the bouquet in the container. This will be the still-life.
4. Place the vase and flowers on the work space next to the white cardboard. Set up the watercolor paints too. Look at the still life. Sketch the shape of the still life lightly with a pencil on the white cardboard.
5. First paint the background of the still life with some kind of neutral or soft, light color of watercolor paints, painting around the shape of the flowers and vase.
6. Next paint the image of the flowers and vase with the watercolor paints. The colors will soak into the white tempera leaving pastel shades and a variety of tones and hues, in the style of the great painter, Renoir.

Pierre-Auguste Renoir

Renoir grew up as a member of a poor working-class family living in Paris. As a teenager, Renoir painted designs on china dishes and ladies' fans to earn money. He was so good that his friends encouraged him to study art as a serious career. Renoir gained in popularity over the years. His paintings were filled with light, fresh colors. "Why shouldn't art be pretty?" he said. "There are enough unpleasant things in the world."

Renoir was a close friend of Claude Monet. They were part of the first Impressionist exhibitions, helping each other and sharing food when money was scarce, as it often was for young unknown artists.

Renoir is best-loved for his paintings of flowers, pretty children, outdoor scenes, and beautiful women. Renoir had a loving family and enjoyed a happy home. In his later years he became crippled with arthritis. When his hands could no longer grasp the paintbrush, he would have the brush tied to his arm so he could continue to paint.

Young artists explore an unusual mixed media activity and achieve the lovely pastel look of a Renoir painting.

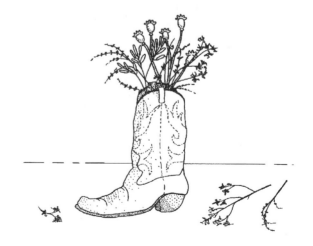

Vincent van Gogh

Vincent van Gogh was not well known during his lifetime, but today he is one of the most famous painters of all time. He only lived a short time but painted approximately 800 pictures. In one of his letters to his brother Theo, he said, "I am functioning like a painting engine." Although he was very ill during the final years of his young life, his last paintings are said to be his best.

He is known for his contrasting colors and his impasto style filled with hatch strokes and rolling, pulsing motions of his paintbrush. Van Gogh would stroke his paint on the canvas with a knife or brush – almost like working with clay – the paint strokes forming marks with textures. One of Vincent van Gogh's most famous paintings is his Sunflowers, rich in color contrasts and impasto painting technique. The impasto painting of Vincent van Gogh is experienced by young artists with a very thick homemade paint with a rough finished texture.

Vincent van Gogh, Sunflowers, 1888

Vincent van Gogh (VAN **GO**) lived only a short time but painted approximately 800 paintings. He was not well known during his lifetime, but today is one of the most famous painters of all time.

Impasto

MATERIALS

- **Impasto Recipe**
  In 1/2 cup of medium thick tempera paint, add one tablespoon of white detergent powder. Stir until mixed. Note: Other thickeners that work well are powdered cornstarch or white flour, using the same 1 T. to 1/2 cup paint.
  Tempera paint thicknesses can vary, so be prepared to thin with water or thicken with more detergent, cornstarch, or flour, if necessary.
- jars or cups for mixing paints
- spoons
- Polystyrene® grocery tray or other flat container
- popsicle stick or tongue depressor
- paintbrushes
- large, white paper or a heavy piece of white posterboard
- tape

PROCESS

1. Prepare the impasto paint recipe in jars or cups, a different color for each container, using spoons, brushes, or popsicle sticks. Van Gogh liked warm colors such as yellow, orange, and brown, but any colors of choice are acceptable for this activity.
2. Scoop dollops of paint colors onto one grocery tray, keeping colors about 1" apart to begin.
3. Apply paint to the paper or posterboard with a popsicle stick or stiff brush. Make textures, lines, and shapes in the paint with the brush or stick.
4. Mix colors together with the stick or a brush on the grocery tray, if desired, to form new colors.
5. Continue to paint and apply more paint until a finished work is complete. The painting will be filled with thick strokes and designs in the paint.
6. Allow the thick impasto painting to dry overnight.

Van Gogh 1853-1890

Van Gogh (VAN GO) tried to express his thoughts and emotions in his paintings, often working days without stopping, spending all of his money on paints, and even forgetting to eat.

Starry Night

MATERIALS
- one sheet of black or dark blue construction paper for the background
- paper scraps
- scissors
- glue
- tempera paints (suggested colors: white, yellow, orange) in jars
- paintbrush
- color print or postcard of van Gogh's painting, *The Starry Night*, optional

PROCESS
Young children may wish to explore making stars with radiating concentric circles. Older children may wish to copy the format of van Gogh's painting with houses, hills, and starry night sky.

1. Mix tempera paint to make very light yellow, white, orange, and darker yellow. Mix each color in a separate jar.
2. To begin, cut the paper scraps into the shapes of little houses, buildings, churches. Glue these in a row along the lower edge of the dark background paper.
3. Next, paint stars in the night sky. Paint a moon too, if desired.
4. For a van Gogh style, paint dots of broken circles around each star and moon (not a solid ring, but 2 or 3 curved brushstrokes that don't quite connect).Then add a second ring of dotted brush strokes around the first ring, moving out from the star into the sky. The stars will begin to look like their sparkles are spilling light into the night sky.
5. Make as many rings around the stars and moon as desired, until the painting has a feeling like one of van Gogh's starry night paintings.

Note: The cover art of *Great Artists* is a starry night painting by Christina Critelli, age 6.

Vincent van Gogh

Van Gogh discovered painting after he had tried and failed at other professions from art dealer to preacher. All of van Gogh's 800 or more paintings were created in the last ten years of his life. He tried to express his thoughts and emotions in his artwork, often working day and night without stopping, spending all of his money on paint, and even forgetting to eat. Van Gogh's paintings are filled with color, swirling images, and intense feelings.

One way that van Gogh showed motion in his work was to make lines of color spreading out into the background, swirling in concentric rings or circles. His paintings show rings of light surrounding stars in a nighttime sky, or radiating from a hot summer sun. The paint looks like ripples made when a stone is tossed into a still puddle. This feeling can be created in a painting of a starry night in the style of Vincent van Gogh.

Christina Critelli, age 6, Starry Night

Cézanne 1839-1906

Paul Cézanne

Cézanne, one of the greatest Post Impressionist painters of all, was a shy man who knew many people but had few friends. Yet, Cézanne worked with many great artists such as the painter, Pissaro, and the writer, Émile Zola. He usually painted "still lifes" – pictures of objects that do not move, like vases, fabrics, plates, and fruits – arranged for display in his studio.

The Post Impressionists and Cézanne came into being at the end of the Impressionist time and are seen as building a bridge from the style of Monet or van Gogh into what we see today as Modern Art. Cézanne developed the style of using geometric shapes as the basis for his paintings because he believed that everything in the world was made up of either a sphere, a cone, a cylinder, or a cube. He formed his designs with strong outlined brush strokes in dark colors, like chiseling shapes into the paint with a carving motion of the paintbrush, a technique that would develop into the well recognized style called Cubism. Like many of the great masters, it was not until after Cézanne's death at age 67 that he received the recognition he deserved as "the father of modern painting".

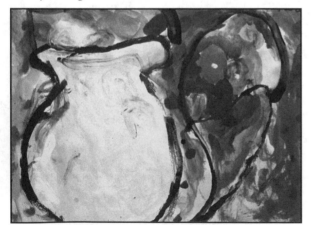

Tara McKinney, age 8, Pitcher with Flowers

*Cézanne (SAY-**ZAHN**) is called "the father of modern painting".*

Seeing Shapes Still-Life

MATERIALS
- still-life item, such as -
  - bowl of fruit   bottle   vase   cup   flower pot
- ruler
- pencil
- stiff paintbrushes
- paper
- tempera paints or acrylic paints in grocery trays or on paper plates
- newspaper covered work area
- painting chisel or other straight edged knife
- postcards or posters of Cézanne's works

PROCESS
1. Look at works of Cézanne, if desired, to see how he uses shapes in his works.
2. Place an item to paint on a table near the artist. Set up the paper and paints. Look at the item and then draw it lightly with pencil on the paper.
3. To achieve a geometric style, take a straight edge ruler and draw on the sketch with strong, straight lines, changing the sketch from rounded to more angular or geometric. Lines can be short, long, or both.
4. Next, dip a chisel or straight edged knife into paint. Dab and cut it onto the pencil lines. Try the same approach with a stiff paintbrush, dabbing or cutting the paint color onto the pencil lines. Use sharp movements. Use as many colors as desired. Make lines as thick as desired.
5. Before the painting is complete, add more paint, but blend, smear, and soften the paints with the tip of the chisel or a paintbrush. This will fill in the geometric shapes somewhat.
6. Dry completely and enjoy looking at the Cézanne-style still-life of geometric shapes.

Rousseau 1844-1910

Once Henri Rousseau (ROO-SO) gave his grandchild an original Rousseau painting and said, "Hold on to this. One day it will be worth a hundred thousand francs." Rousseau was right!

Jungle Prints

MATERIALS
- several flat leaves and ferns
- tempera paint
- brayer, or a homemade paint roller (see directions below)
- flat pan or cookie sheet
- white drawing paper
- lots of scrap paper
- paintbrush

PROCESS
1. Place a puddle of green paint on the flat pan and roll it with the brayer. The side of a jar or a small rolling pin can be used instead.
2. Hold a leaf by its stem on top of a sheet of scrap paper. Gently roll the paint-covered brayer on top of the leaf. Roll several times, always in an upward direction, until the leaf is covered with a thin coat of paint. Roll the brayer in the pan often to re-color it. Add more paint to the pan if it's needed. Then set aside.
3. Carefully place the leaf, paint side down, on a sheet of white drawing paper. Lay a clean piece of scrap paper on top and pat it gently. Don't let the leaf wiggle. Lift the paper and the leaf stem to see the leaf print made beneath.
4. Print several more leaves on the paper using different tones of green (light green with some white paint mixed in, dark green with black mixed in, yellow green, olive green, blue green, or any other greens). Make greens by mixing colors of paint as they are rolled on the pan with the brayer. Print all the leaves growing up from the bottom of the paper, as if they were jungle trees.
5. After the leaf prints dry, use a paintbrush to add flowers, fruit, jungle animals, or even people into the leafy scene.
6. Dry completely. Hang on the wall, if desired, to view the Rousseau-style jungle print.

Henri Rousseau

The great painter Henri Rousseau never studied to be an artist and did not start painting until late in his life. He painted jungle scenes purely from imagination, never actually leaving France to visit the exotic places found in his paintings. Some people called Rousseau's paintings simple and even made fun of them, especially the art critics in 1900 in Paris. Rousseau was very popular with other artists and always had confidence in himself. No matter what the art critics said, Rousseau knew his work was good. Once he gave his grandchild a painting he made and said, "Hold on to this. One day it will be worth a hundred thousand francs." Rousseau was almost right because his paintings are worth far more than that. Today his paintings are shown in the greatest museums of the world.

Rousseau is best known for his paintings of jungle scenes, with a canvas full of hundreds of thick green leaves, flowers, and tropical animals. Young artists create a jungle picture in the style of Rousseau with an easy printmaking technique.

Peter James, age 8, Jungle

Rodin 1840-1917

Auguste Rodin

Francois Auguste Rene Rodin grew up in Paris. He wanted to be an artist, but although he went to a school for craftsmen and worked as a stonecutter, he could not get accepted at the famous School of Fine Arts. When Rodin was 22, he entered a monastery. The abbot of the order recognized Rodin's talents and encouraged him to become a sculptor.

Rodin worked hard studying artists of the past and creating sculptures. He became one of the greatest sculptors in the world. The figures in Rodin's statues are realistic and very strong, but Rodin did not want to sculpt perfect people. One of his earliest works is called "Man with a Broken Nose," a rugged portrait of a beat-up old boxer. At first the galleries would not exhibit the piece, not until they changed its name to " Portrait of a Roman".

Rodin made his statues of metal and carved stone. The young artist can explore Rodin's style by carving in soft modeling clay.

Rodin (RO-DAN) did not want to sculpt perfect people. He liked to sculpt statues that were realistic and strong. One of his earliest works is called "Man with a Broken Nose," a rugged portrait of a beat-up old boxer.

Carving Clay

MATERIALS

- 1 or 2 lb. of modeling clay or Plasticine
- wire loop carving tools made with paperclips, wooden clothespins, and masking tape to hold

PROCESS

1. Make 2 or 3 wire loop carving tools with rounded or pointed tips. To do this, straighten a paperclip, then bend it into the desired shape. Pinch the ends of the paperclip wire with a wooden clothespin. Then wrap the end of the clothespin tightly with masking tape to hold it shut. (See illustration.)

2. Mold the clay into a ball or lump roughly the shape of the sculpture desired. Some suggestions are:
    - animals, like a sleeping cat or dog, a fat hippo, or an owl
    - a human head (in art, called a bust)
    - abstract sculpture that is simply a design and not realistic

   Note: Creatures with long necks or thin legs will be too delicate for clay carving.

3. Once the clay is molded into a rough shape, do not pinch or model it any more. Instead, use a wire tool to carve away tiny strips of clay. Try to imagine that the clay is a chunk of solid stone. Once a chunk is carved off, it can't be put back, so work slowly and carefully while sculpting the figure or design. Work until satisfied with the sculpture.

4. Modeling clay stays soft, so put the finished sculpture where it won't get squished.

VARIATION

- For a sculpture that hardens, purchase clay products at hobby or art stores, such as -
    - Playdough or DAS™ that dries hard in the air
    - Sculpey™ clay that can be baked hard in an oven
    - pottery clay (Moist Clay™) that can be fired hard in a kiln or left to air dry

Gauguin 1848-1903

Gauguin (GO-GAN) used color in entirely new ways in his paintings. He might paint a sky yellow, grass orange, and mountains red.

Surprising Colors

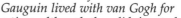

MATERIALS
- tempera paints in bright colors
- paintbrushes
- large sheet of drawing paper
- wide masking tape
- work table

PROCESS
1. Assemble the paints, brushes, and paper.
2. Place the paper on the table. Tape the paper to the table with masking tape as pictured in the illustration. When the tape is peeled off later, it will leave a natural frame around the painting.
3. Think of a landscape to paint such as a mountain, lake, and trees.
4. Think of colors opposite to the real colors.
5. Paint the painting with colors that are opposite and not real. For example, paint the grass pink instead of green, the lake yellow instead of blue, the sky purple instead of blue, and so on. Use broad, flat lines and colors.
6. Allow the painting to dry.
7. Gently peel away the masking tape. A frame will be left around the Gauguin style painting of unusual colors.

Paul Gauguin

   The French artist, Paul Gauguin, is famous for using unusual colors in his paintings of everyday things, people, and nature. Gauguin was a sailor for many years, and then became a stock broker in Paris. After taking art lessons, he quit his job and became an artist full time. Gauguin lived with van Gogh for a time, although they didn't get along very well. Gauguin left and traveled to the South Seas and Tahiti where he would eventually make his home for the rest of his life. The beauty of Tahiti inspired Gauguin to paint most of his famous beautiful works. He painted in flat, bright colors, showing the lives of the native Tahitians. This is where he began to experiment with color in his paintings. Gauguin might paint a sky yellow, grass orange, and mountains red.

   Young artists can experiment with unusual colors in a simple landscape painting using bright tempera paints.

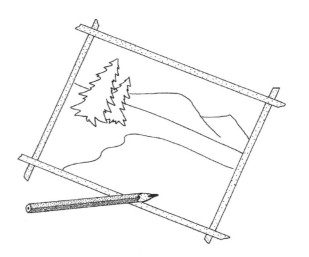

Toulouse-Lautrec 1864-1901

*As a child, Toulouse-Lautrec (TOO-**LOOZ** LAH-**TREK**) loved drawing and horseback riding. When his legs were severely injured during his teen years, he discovered he had a magnificent artistic talent that would become his career and his life.*

Event Poster

MATERIALS
- large sheet of brown craft paper, torn from a roll, cut to about 3'x5'
- tempera paints in cups, especially white, black, and red (as well as other colors)
- paintbrushes
- wall
- tacks or tape
- newspaper

PROCESS
1. Tape or tack the corners of the large sheet of brown craft paper to the wall. Line newspaper on the floor to catch any drips from the brown paper. Set up the paints in cups on the newspaper by the brown paper.
2. Think of a special event to advertise with this large poster. For example, a pet show, parade, puppet show, school play, or birthday party would work well.
3. Paint the outline of a person, perhaps someone at a birthday party having a grand time, with white. Then, paint in parts of the person with black and other colors. Leave parts unpainted. For example, paint the hair, face, and hat of a person, but leave the clothes outlined in white.
4. Add other sketchy painted bits and parts to the poster. Add words, if desired, such as, Amy's Exciting Party. With a paintbrush, sign the artist's name.
5. When the poster is dry, post it in a place where everyone will see it and want to come to the special event.

Toulouse-Lautrec, Moulin Rouge La Goulue, 1891

Toulouse-Lautrec continued

Kyle Casteel, age 8, Birthday Poster

Henri de Toulouse-Lautrec

Henri de Toulouse-Lautrec was a French Impressionist painter who dealt with a severe leg deformity. Toulouse-Lautrec's legs were never normal after an illness or an accident in his teen years. While the rest of his family was riding horses, he began to discover he had a magnificent artistic talent that would become his career and his life. Toulouse-Lautrec especially loved to draw horses and drew them all over the margins of his school notebooks. As he grew older, he spent time at the circus, noisy French cafés, carnivals, shows, and town performances drawing the people and animals in colorful Impressionistic works of art. He is well known for painting over 300 posters to advertise performances in his favorite cafés and theaters. The critics of the day did not think much of his work, but today, Toulouse-Lautrec is thought to be one of the great artistic geniuses of all time.

In Toulouse-Lautrec's posters announcing shows or events, he would outline his models or subjects with broad paint lines, and then only partially fill in the work with more paint. This style would highlight portions of the poster to capture the attention of a passersby. Young artists explore Toulouse-Lautrec's idea of making a poster to advertise a special event in this painting activity on brown craft paper.

Seurat 1859-1891

Georges Seurat

Georges Seurat was a French Impressionist painter who invented a special style of painting called Pointillism. Seurat painted pictures using tiny dots of paint color instead of regular brush strokes and solid areas of color. He made different shades of color by painting dots of pure colors close to each other. In this way, he created green by mixing blue and yellow dots. Browns and golds were made with tiny dots of red, blue and orange.

Seurat's most famous painting is titled Sunday Afternoon on the Island of La Grande Jatte. *The picture shows a park with dozens of people walking and relaxing in the grass beneath shady trees. Close up, the canvas is covered with thousands of tiny dots of paint. To see the picture, one must step back and look at it from a distance. Then the dots of pure color blend together to create a shimmering scene. La Grande Jatte is a huge painting 7 feet tall and nearly 10 feet across. Seurat worked on this one painting for nearly two years, inventing dot combinations for every shade of color in the scene. He discovered that tiny dots of orange scattered in with other colors gave the impression of sparkling sunlight. The young artist invents colors, too, just like Seurat.*

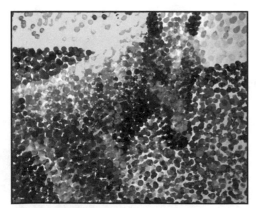

Nici Smith, age 12, Horse of Dots

*Georges Seurat (SOO-**RAH**) invented a special style of painting called Pointillism using only tiny dots of paint and no brush strokes or lines.*

Pointillist Color Cards

MATERIALS
- tempera paints in 5 colors: red, yellow, blue, white and black
- cotton-swabs (Q-tips)
- white 3" x 5" index cards
- white drawing paper

PROCESS
1. Pour a selection of paints into 5 small dishes. Do not mix the paints together. Leave them as pure colors, one in each dish. Put a cotton swab in each dish.
2. To practice and understand Pointillism, cover four index cards with red dots. Dab the red cotton swab onto the card, over and over, dipping it back in the red paint as necessary. Let the red dots dry completely.
3. When the dots are dry, add dots of another paint color to one of the red dot cards. Make one card with red and yellow dots. Make another card with red and blue dots, and so on. Prop the painted cards up and look at them from across the room. Do the dots mix together to make different colors?
4. Make many different dot cards. Try to use dots of pure color, letting the paint dry between each color so the wet paint doesn't mix together too much. Many different colors can be made. Try to create a brown shades, or pink, or sky blue, or green.
5. Now paint an entire picture with colored dots in the style of Seurat. Sometimes it helps to sketch a picture on white paper with pencil and then paint it using dots of pure color touched on the paper with cotton swabs. To make really small dots, cut the cotton off the swab and use only the cardboard stick end of the swab.

Vuillard 1868-1940

Vuillard's (VOOE-YAHRD) paintings on canvas captured beauty indoors.

Artist's Studio

MATERIALS
- paint easel
- newspaper to cover the floor under the easel
- large paper on easel board
- jar of clear water
- indoor scene
- rag
- tempera paints in cups, mixed as low-tone colors (rather than bright colors)
- paintbrushes
- soft, drawing pencil or charcoal

PROCESS
1. Set up a paint easel on top of newspapers. Attach a large sheet of paper to the easel. Prepare the cups of tempera paint and place in the easel tray. Place a paintbrush in each color of paint. Place a jar of clear water in the easel tray for rinsing brushes. Hang a rag on the easel tray for drying brushes or wiping drips. This painting area can be called the studio.

2. Set up the easel so it allows the artist to view the room – the studio. Then look about the room. Decide on what scene to paint. For example, if several people are sitting at a table enjoying a cookie and milk, this might be a good scene to paint. Or, the layout of a corner of the room with chairs, lamp, and a pot of flowers might be another scene to paint. It might also work to ask someone to model and sit or stand as part of a scene.

3. Once the scene is selected, quickly sketch the scene on the large paper with a soft drawing pencil or a piece of charcoal. Then, begin painting. Paint the scene in any way desired. Note: Tempera paints work well for exploring the style of Vuillard because they create a flat surface of paint with broad, simple detail. The low-tone paint colors will add to Vuillard's style of painting. During the painting process, brushes can be rinsed and dried as needed.

4. When the painting is complete, allow it to dry completely before moving or displaying. Remember to clean up the studio when done!

Édouard Vuillard

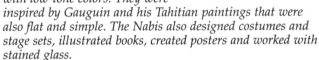

Vuillard was a shy man who lived a quiet life, exhibiting his works only until he turned 45 years old. He was a French painter and part of a small group of artists who called themselves the Nabis, exhibiting together from 1891-1900. The Nabis style stressed flat lines and patterns with low-tone colors. They were inspired by Gauguin and his Tahitian paintings that were also flat and simple. The Nabis also designed costumes and stage sets, illustrated books, created posters and worked with stained glass.

The Nabis felt that a picture – before being a person or a subject – was a flat surface covered with colors arranged in a certain order. Vuillard liked to arrange his colors on a flat surface to show interior scenes, richly colored but low-toned, often painting his quiet, personal surroundings. He captured beauty indoors in his studio.

Young artists set up an art studio with a paint easel just like Vuillard, capturing the beauty of their own indoor surroundings on common newsprint.

Russell 1864-1926

C.M. Russell

Charles Marion Russell was an American painter and sculptor famous for his scenes of life in the wild West and the cowboys and people who lived there. As a child he loved to draw and model animals, cowboys, and Indians. Russell taught himself art and never took any lessons. Because he was interested in the West, his parents allowed him to travel to the territory of Montana when he was only 16. He made Montana his lifetime home.

Russell experienced authentic western life for his artwork. He lived with the Blood Indian tribe in Canada for an entire winter, worked as a hunter for 2 years, and worked as a cowboy for 10 years. Eventually he gave up cowboy life and began painting and sculpting full-time. His work shows action and detail, with authentic backgrounds and settings. He was equally skilled in oil paint, pen-and-ink, watercolor, and clay.

Young artists may not be able to live a cowboy life like Russell, but they can imagine the Montana sunsets Russell saw by observing sunsets in their own skies and painting one on paper. Add a silhouette and a western sunset scene is complete.

*Because Russell (**RUH**-SUHL) was a working cowboy, he painted authentic western life in his artworks.*

Western Sunset

MATERIALS
- tempera or watercolor paints
- water in a jar
- paintbrushes
- rag
- sheet of white paper
- black paper
- scissors
- pencil
- paste or glue

PROCESS
1. Observe a sunset some evening. Notice where the darkest and brightest colors are. Notice where the lightest and faintest colors are. Notice colors in the clouds.
2. Choose paints that are close to the colors observed in the sunset. Assemble them with brushes, clear water for rinsing, and a rag for clean-up. Note: If a blurred, softened and blended sunset is desired, first dampen the white paper with clear water from a paintbrush. If a bold sunset is desired, work on dry paper.
3. Paint a sunset. Think of painting colorful clouds and where to put the darker, bolder colors and where to put the fainter, lighter colors. Fill the entire painting with a sunset. While the sunset painting is drying, get out the black paper, a pencil and scissors.
4. Think of a western scene, or any scene. For example, imagine a cactus, a cowboy on a horse, hills or desert, a mining shack, a scraggly tree. Sketch with the pencil and cut out with scissors – or cut free-hand – this western scene from black paper. These cuttings will be silhouettes and will not need any details like doorknobs, leaves, faces, etc. Simply cut the shape out, like an outline or a shadow filled in with black paper.
5. Next, cut a silhouette strip of paper that will go across the bottom of the entire painting to represent the ground or earth in the scene. (See illustration for help with the silhouette placement.) Paste the black silhouette on the sunset painting.

Megan Kohl, age 7, Sunset

WILD & WACKY

Expressionists, Abstract, Abstract-Expressionists, Cubists, Dadaists, & Surrealists

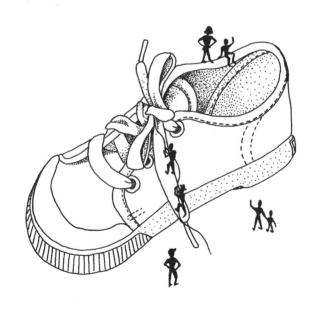

Matisse 1869-1954

Henri Matisse

Henri Matisse, a French artist who made bright, joyful paper collages in simple shapes, became famous as the leader of a new style of art called Post Impressionism which featured a new way to paint and express feelings. Because these strange shapes and bright colors were shocking, the style was called "fauvism" which means "wild beast" in French, because the new Post Impressionistic art was so wild and expressive.

Matisse loved simple contrasting colors and believed they could tell stories. For instance, Matisse used blue to show truth or heaven, orange to show love or gentleness, red to show excitement or fire, and green to show growth or change. Part of the enjoyment of looking at the work of Matisse is trying to understand what stories he was telling through his art. Young artists cut or tear colored paper and create a work of colored paper shapes that may tell a story or may simply imitate the style of the great Post Impressionist, Henri Matisse.

David Royce, age 7, cut paper

Matisse (MAH-TEESS) painted with strange shapes and bright colors that were thought shocking in his day – a style called "fauvism" (which means "wild beast" in French), because his work was so wild and expressive.

Story Color Collage

MATERIALS
- scraps of colored paper, such as -
  bright art tissues, construction paper, origami paper, pieces of fingerpaintings cut into scraps
- white glue thinned with water in a dish with paintbrush
- other glues of choice, such as glue sticks or glue in squeeze bottle
- scissors
- masking tape
- poster board

PROCESS
1. Collect an assortment of colored papers. Select some that go together or contrast nicely. Glue some larger squares or rectangles of color on the paper as a background. Art tissues painted on with thinned glue will give a transparent bright effect. Other papers work well too.
2. Next, cut some of the papers into interesting shapes. To imitate Matisse, the shapes should be bold and simple in their designs. Glue the shapes on the background papers of the collage. Add more shapes in black or deeper colors to give centers of interest to the collage, if desired.
3. To express a story, decide on what the colors and shapes of the paper will symbolize. Then glue them on the collage in a way that expresses feelings or tells a story like a colorful dreamlike photograph. For example, the arrival of a new baby might be shown with a bright pink rounded shape in the center of other colors (the adults surrounding the baby). The ideas for this type of expression are completely up to the artist.
4. Allow the collage to dry.

Munch 1863-1944

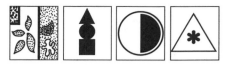

Munch (MOONCH) expressed his sad childhood through his Expressionist paintings.

Clay Facial Expressions

MATERIALS
- playdough, plasticine, clay, or other modeling compound
- work area for clay (Use individual large rectangular scraps of formica as a portable work surface for each child. Individual boards work well too.)
- tempera paints in deep colors, paper, and brushes, optional

PROCESS
1. Work a large lump of modeling clay until it is smooth and elastic.
2. Place the clay on the work surface and mold it into an oval face shape.
3. Squeeze, poke, and pull facial features into the clay oval. Pull the features from the oval without adding or attaching any extra clay pieces. Try to make a happy face with happy arched eyebrows and a smiling mouth. Then, experiment with changing the face into a sad face by turning down the corners of the smile and lifting the center corners of the eyebrows. Try other expressions such as frightened, crying, sleeping, surprised, adorable and sweet, or lonely. All of these expressions can be explored in clay by pulling, poking, and squeezing the clay.
4. When done, put the clay away for use at another time. Clean the work board.
5. As a follow-up, explore painting facial expressions with deep colors of tempera paint on paper.

VARIATION
- Work with a mirror propped up next to the clay project so the artist can make different expressions in the mirror and then capture them in clay.

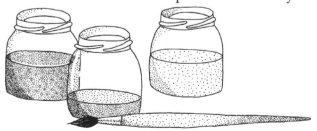

Edvard Munch

Edvard Munch was born in Norway and studied briefly in Paris. He had a very sad childhood because his mother and sister both died very young. This sadness became part of his Expressionist artworks. His most famous painting is called "The Scream", which shows the skull-like face of Munch framed on either side by his hands over his ears. The scream from Munch's face appears to carry off through the river and the sunset into the landscape with a dizzying effect of swirling paint in deep colors.

Munch was greatly influenced by the Impressionists as seen in his highly expressive paintings around the 1890's and early 1900's. He is known as an Expressionist and shows this in his works especially through facial expressions. The young artist can explore different kinds of facial expressions by working with clay or other modeling compound.

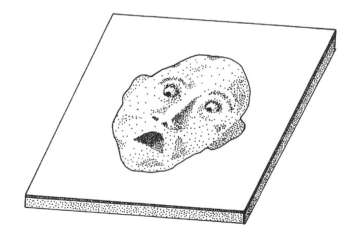

Kandinsky 1866-1944

Wassily Kandinsky

Wassily Kandinsky took music and art lessons as a child in Russia, but he did not become a professional artist until he was 30 years old. He gave up his job as a law professor and moved to Germany to study art. In those days, people thought that a drawing or painting had to look like its subject – the more realistic, the better.

The Impressionist painters started to paint pictures that didn't look exactly real. Kandinsky was the first artist to take the final step away from realism: he painted the first totally abstract pictures, paintings that were pure designs, and believed that colors and forms had meanings all their own. He was a musician as well as a painter, and thought of colors as music. Simple pictures were like little melodies to him. Complex paintings were like symphonies. He called many of his paintings "Improvisations", meaning a song made up on the spot, not planned ahead of time.

Young artists can enjoy the music of colors by letting imaginations fly while painting to music!

*Kandinsky (CAN-**DIN**-SKEE) believed that simple pictures were like little melodies and complex paintings were like grand symphonies.*

Painting Music

MATERIALS
- watercolors, tempera or acrylic paints
- paintbrushes
- paper, matte board or canvas board
- source of music, on tapes, CD's, or records

PROCESS
1. Select a special piece of music. These well-known classical pieces are great for painting. A librarian will help order and check out cassette tapes from a public library. Any kind of music is for painting, from contemporary rock music to jazz or traditional music from around the world to children's favorite sing-alongs.
   - Bach - *Brandenberg Concertos*
   - Wagner - *The Ride of the Valkyries*
   - Ravel - *Bolero*
   - Copeland - *Appalachian Spring*
   - Saint-Sens - *Danse Macabre*
   - Grofe - *Grand Canyon Suite*
2. Listen to the music selection for 5 or 10 minutes without doing anything else with eyes closed. Stretch out on the floor, if desired. Try to imagine what colors, lines and shapes can be used to show the feelings that the music creates.
3. Now listen to the music again while painting a picture of the sounds. Use lines, shapes and colors without trying to draw any particular object. Create an abstract design that is made up on the spot – an improvisation created without planning or sketching ahead of time.
4. Change the music selection and paint again. Look at the different results to different kinds of music.

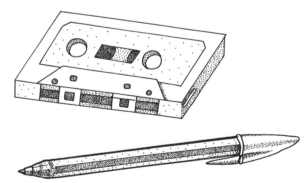

Mondrian 1872-1944

*Mondrian (**MOHN**-DREE-UN) wanted to create pictures to express thoughts and feelings entirely created with straight lines and simple colors.*

Straight Line Design

MATERIALS
- 9"x12" (or larger) piece of graph paper with large squares
- glue
- matte board or cardboard
- choice of tape or markers, such as -
    - black electrician's tape   colored masking tape
    - black marking pen   strips of black construction paper
- ruler, optional
- scissors
- choice of coloring tools, such as -
    - paints and brushes   crayons   colored pencils   colored markers

PROCESS
1. Glue the graph paper to a piece of matte board or cardboard to make it strong. Dry completely before beginning the project.
2. Divide the graph paper into different sized squares and rectangles with strips of black tape. Start by taping all around the edges. Then tape across the paper. Then cut shorter lengths of tape to divide some of the inside squares. To keep the design in the spirit of Mondrian's work, make all the lines straight up and down or across, following the faint lines of the graph paper. If black tape is not available, divide the paper by drawing black marker pen lines with a ruler or coloring in squares to make long black lines. Strips of black construction paper could also be used. Colored masking tape would also work, although Mondrian's works are known for the black dividing lines.
3. Turn the tape design different ways to find out which way the design looks the best.
4. Color or paint a few of the white areas in the design. Mondrian liked to use bright colors like red, blue and yellow. Some of the areas can be left white and unpainted.

Piet Mondrian

   Piet Mondrian grew up in Holland. After he finished his regular schooling, he studied to be an artist. Following a visit to Paris in 1910, Mondrian stopped drawing and painting real-life landscapes and portraits of people. He turned instead to abstract images – geometric designs that did not have any particular subject or name.

   Mondrian wanted to create pictures to express thoughts and feelings. Mondrian worked hard to find just the right placement of lines to make squares and rectangles. He wanted to create a design that felt just right, with perfect harmony between the lines and colors. His most famous paintings are made entirely of straight lines and simple colors, like the simplest form of Cubism possible.

   Young children can create a Mondrian-style design on graph paper – the straight lines in place as a guide.

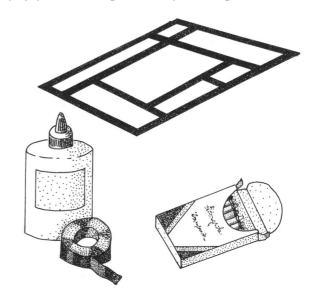

Paul Klee

Paul Klee came from a musical family and lived a musical life. He was born in Switzerland to a German father who was a church organist. Klee was a trained violinist and studied music in Germany and considered himself German. It was hard for him to decide between a career in art or music, but he chose art. Klee's wife was a piano teacher. Because he didn't have an art studio, he painted at his kitchen table while his wife taught piano lessons. During these years his drawings, etchings, and watercolors were small due to the size of his table. Later on, he lived in a two-family house where he had his first art studio. Klee's neighbor in the other half of the house was Kandinsky (the artist famous for paintings that are like music). Kandinsky and Klee were good friends and respected each other's work, but did not have any particular artistic influence on each other.

Because Klee (KLAY) didn't have an art studio, he painted at his kitchen table. His drawings, etchings, and watercolors were small due to the size of his little kitchen table.

One Line Designs

MATERIALS
- white drawing paper
- pencil and eraser
- black permanent ink marking pen
  (Caution: The black ink in a permanent marker will not wash out of clothing or off hands and furniture.)
- watercolor paints and paintbrush
- 10 feet or more of lightweight wire, such as plastic coated electrical wire, copper or brass wire from a hardware store
- a lump of clay that will air dry hard, such as playdough or DAS™ modeling compound

PROCESS
One Line Realistic Drawing
1. With a pencil, lightly sketch an object on white drawing paper. Draw any simple object, such as the following ideas:

a face	vase of flowers	race car
pet sitting	house	tree

2. Draw over the pencil sketch with a black permanent marker, again without lifting the pen off the paper until the whole picture is finished. Let the continuous line cross over itself and loop from one area to another until the single line has drawn the entire object.
3. Then completely erase all the underlying pencil lines with a soft eraser that won't tear the paper.
   Hint: A soft art gum eraser from a hobby or art store works well.
4. Decorate some areas in the drawing with watercolor paints, leaving other areas unpainted. Let dry.

Hannah Kohl, age 8, One Line Cat and House
One Line Realistic Drawing

Klee continued

One Line Abstract Design

1. Place the point of the permanent marker on one corner of a sheet of drawing paper. Then slowly and carefully, without lifting the pen up, let the pen wander all over the paper. Make long lines, tiny loops, zig zags, and swirls. Leave some parts of the paper open and white, without any lines. Make other areas dense with lines. Create an abstract design in any way desired.

2. When the line ink drawing is finished, use watercolor paints to color some of the areas in the design. Leave other spaces white.
   Note: Using a permanent marker prevents the wet paint from dissolving the black ink line like it would if normal water-based marking pens were used.

One Line Sculpture

1. A single continuous line of wire can also create a sculpture—a three dimensional artwork that can be seen from all different sides. Carefully bend a single length of thin wire this way and that to make a pleasing shape. Create an abstract design or bend the wire to resemble an actual object.

2. For a permanent standing sculpture, stick the ends of the wire into a lump of clay or dough to hold. When the clay dries hard, place the wire sculpture on a shelf or table to view.

Klee was deeply interested in the art of children and tried to capture the creativity of children's art in his own paintings. Klee felt children's art held mysteries about creativity. Like some children, he often drew with a scratchy line and soft tones, often working on paper no bigger than a sheet of notebook paper. He often combined colorful paintings with line drawings, sometimes incorporating hieroglyphics in his art. Klee's artworks are called poetic; that is, his paintings are like poems to be held in the hand and read, rather than pictures to be hung on the wall and viewed. Klee's paintings and drawings combine folk art, abstract art, and humor. Many of his images have titles that make us smile. One of his earliest pen and ink drawings is called "Two Men Meet, Each Believing the Other to Be of Higher Rank." Another famous Klee painting showing simple bird shapes on a wire is called "The Twittering Machine."

Young artists explore Klee's style with a type of drawing called "One Line Design" which means never lifting the pen from the paper while creating a drawing with one connected line that goes on and on.

Jenny Lemon, Age 7, Wiggly Watercolor
One Line Abstract Design

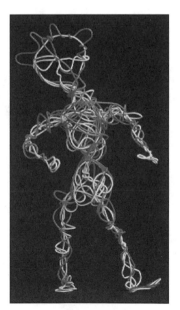

Nici Smith, Age 10,
Wire Man
One Line Sculpture

Stella 1880-1946

Joseph Stella
Joseph Stella was born in Italy and grew up in the United States. Not much is recorded about his years growing up, but as an adult he is well known for line art and mixed media. Mixed media is any combination of art materials, such as paint, crayons, collage, and colored pencils. Many artists only use one art material, so it is interesting to explore the style of Stella and try using two or more media all in one artwork.

Stella considered himself a Futurist. Futurists tried to show movement through repetition of an image in a painting and also believed that artists should not paint the figure or object, but should paint the shapes and atmosphere around the object. There was a fascination with geometric precision, engineering, machines, and architecture. Stella created works in his special style with lines and spaces.

To imitate Stella's Futurist style, the young artist will need a ruler, marking pen, and crayons or other coloring tools. The results of this art exploration are dramatic and will highlight a definite center of interest in the young artist's design.

Joseph Stella (STEH-LUH) was fascinated with geometric shapes, lines, and mixed media.

Mixed Media Lines

MATERIALS
- paper
- black marking pen
- straight edge
- paints and brushes
- colored chalk
- crayons
- black tempera paint and brush

PROCESS
1. Draw a black dot with the marking pen somewhere on the white paper. It does not need to be in the center. It can be anywhere.
2. Next, use a straight edge or ruler to draw lines with a black marking pen out from the dot to the edge of the paper, like the sun's rays shining out. For the drawing to resemble Stella's style, draw at least 3 lines or as many as 12 lines.
3. Color-in some of the spaces between the lines with colored chalks. Color other spaces with crayons.
4. Next, paint over the black lines again with thick, black tempera to separate the sections more and to accentuate the lines. Dry completely.

VARIATION
- Draw big, loopy swirls instead of straight lines with a black marking pen. Fill in the spaces with color, lines, designs, or patterns. Paint over the entire design with a black wash (black paint thinned with water) to create a loopy crayon resist.

Escher 1889-1972

*Escher (**ESH**-ER) was a genius at creating tessellations and for his design patterns of lizards, birds, and fish that are simply amazing!*

Tessellation Design

MATERIALS
- heavy paper for the pattern
- square shape to trace (box lid, block, etc.)
- eraser
- crayons, colored pencils or colored markers
- sheet of background paper
- pencil
- scissors
- pieces of colored paper
- glue

PROCESS
1. Start by drawing a square on heavy paper. Change the line on one side of the square by adding a wiggle or a bump. Then change the top of the square in some way too. Cut this square out. It will be the main tessellation pattern.
2. Lightly trace the pattern square over and over on the pieces of colored paper. Make any number, but more than four. Cut out the colored squares. Now there are weird shapes that will fit together perfectly: side to side and top to bottom.
3. Glue these colored squares touching each other on the background paper to create a tessellation. Squares can be flipped over before gluing.
4. The tessellation can be a geometric pattern, or with imagination, it could be turned into a picture of something. The shape in the example on this page reminded the artist of a dog, so he added a nose and eye, whiskers and a collar. Result - a tessellating puppy!

RESOURCE
- Find great tessellations designed by kids in a book titled *Tessellation Winners*, Dale Seymour Publications. This publisher sponsors a yearly contest for student tessellation designs. To enter this contest, write to Dale Seymour Publications, PO Box 10888, Palo Alto, CA 94303. Dale Seymour also has a book called *Introduction to Tessellations*, with everything there is to know about these amazing designs!

M.C. Escher

A tessellation is a special kind of design made from shapes that fit together perfectly. A checkerboard is a simple tessellation made of squares. Other shapes can make a tessellation too. Some triangles, rectangles, and diamonds fit together perfectly. The fun really starts when weird shapes are used to make a tessellation.

M.C. Escher grew up in Holland in the early years of the 20th Century. He studied art and traveled through Europe as a young man. During his travels he discovered that he especially liked the geometric designs made by Moorish artists in Spain and northern Africa.

Escher was a genius at creating tessellations. He designed patterns with lizards, birds, and fish that are simply amazing! Young artists experience designing a tessellation with drawing and coloring tools and tracing paper.

Ashley Cole, age 6, Tesselating Puppy, inspired from a Dale Seymour tessella

Calder 1889-1976

Alexander Calder

Alexander Calder was an American sculptor who first trained as a design engineer, not as a sculptor. Calder is most famous for originating the sculpture technique called "mobile", or art that moves. Calder's mobiles were sometimes several feet long from one end to the other and were carefully balanced constructions of metal plates, wires, and rods which are moved by the air or by the help of a gentle push of the hand. The movement makes them a continually moving and changing design.

As a child, Calder enjoyed making things from old dishes and pieces of wire. He also loved to make contraptions from his collections of scraps and junk. Mobiles make use of scraps and junk, too. They can hang from the ceiling or stand freely. In this project, a stand-up mobile is made from a Styrofoam™ packing block for the base and wire for the structure of the mobile.

*When Calder (**CAHL**-DER) was a child, he enjoyed creating things from old dishes and pieces of wire, and making contraptions from his collections of scraps and junk.*

Standing Mobile

MATERIALS
- craft wire (telephone cable colored wire also works well)
- Styrofoam™ packing block
- bits of paper, foil, stickers
- glue or tape
- scissors

PROCESS
1. Cut craft wire to any length desired.
2. Stick the wire into the top of the block of Styrofoam™. The wire can be bent into wiggly shapes or left straight.
3. Add more wire in the block.
4. Tape or glue bits of paper to the wires like flags or flower blossoms. Stickers work well too.
5. Add more wire and paper bits as needed.
6. The free-standing mobile will move in the air currents or when placed near an open window. The gentle push of a finger can set the mobile in motion, too.

VARIATIONS
- Hang the Styrofoam™ block with wires and paper bits upside down from the ceiling.
- Add other lightweight materials to the mobile such as thread, beads, and confetti.

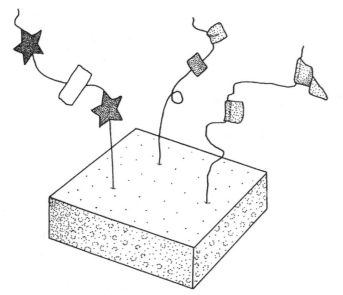

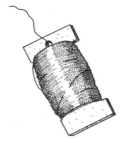

Moore 1898-1986

Moore's (MOR) sculptures are like strange, ancient rocks eroded by time and weather.

Carving Stone

MATERIALS
- sawdust or old cornflakes
- plaster of Paris
- disposable mixing container
- stirring stick
- small paper milk carton with the top cut off
- old spoon and other simple carving tools
- scrap newspapers to cover the work area
- water

PROCESS

1. Mix equal parts of sawdust and plaster of Paris in the plastic container.
   Note: Do not breathe the plaster dust.

2. Stir enough water into the plaster and sawdust until the mixture is like a thick gravy. Too little water will leave a mixture that is too stiff and dry. Too much water will make a mixture that is watery and thin.

3. Quickly pour the thick mixture into the milk carton. Work fast, because the plaster begins to harden in just a few minutes. Dispose of the mixing container and any extra plaster mixture in the trash can. Do not rinse this mixture or its scrapings down the sink or it might seriously clog the drain.

4. After about an hour, the mixture will be solid and the paper milk carton can be torn away. Inside will be a lump of "stone", which will feel damp and warm from the chemical reaction that made the plaster harden.

5. Next, use a spoon and other tools to carve into the soft stone by gently scraping away the surface. Do not use any good metal tools to carve the "stone" because the plaster might ruin them. Try to make an abstract shape or realistic sculpture. A realistic sculpture might be a statue of an animal or a fish.

6. After a few days, the stone will become completely hard and dry.
   Note: It's easiest to work the stone the first day when it is still damp and soft, but can be carved even after it is dried.

Henry Moore

The British sculptor Henry Moore created smooth, rounded sculptures and statues out of carved wood and rock. Many of his statues look like humans and families. Others are graceful abstract shapes. To some people, Moore's sculptures appear to be eroded by a thousand years of wind and water. Carving real stone takes special tools and lots of hard work. Young artists create a sculpture that looks like carved stone, yet is so soft it can be carved with a spoon!

Braque 1882-1963

Georges Braque

Georges Braque began his young painter's life as an exterior house painter working for his father in a small town in France. He later moved to Paris where he studied at the free Academie Humbert where he began his interest in art as a career.

Cubism was almost entirely invented by the two artists and friends, Braque and Piccasso. Braque became a Cubist painter and was one of the first artists to experiment with looking at shapes as geometric and abstract, often presenting several views at the same time. These shapes could be cut and then pasted within a painting or cut and pasted on their own. Sometimes printed paper or other objects were glued into the paintings.

The young artist experiments with a Cubist approach by tearing paper into squarish shapes which can then be glued into a collage and combined with painting.

Davin LaRue, age 5, Paper Shapes

Georges Braque (BRAHK) began his young painter's life as a house painter working for his father in a small town in France.

Cubist Collage

MATERIALS
- select a paper for the background, in any color
- colored paper to tear into squares and other geometric shapes
- other papers to tear into squares and shapes, such as -
  - wrapping paper
  - wrapping tissue
  - photos
  - junk mail
  - pictures from magazines or catalogs
  - art tissue
  - newspaper
  - facial tissues or paper towels
  - old posters or book covers
- white glue, thinned slightly with water, in a dish
- paintbrush to use with glue
- tempera paints
- paintbrushes
- newspaper covered work space

PROCESS
1. Spread out a selection of favorite papers on the work space. Choose a piece of paper and tear away a piece into a square or other geometric shape.
2. Glue it on the background paper.
3. Now tear another paper into a square or shape and glue this on the background paper too. Tear and glue as many shapes as desired.
4. Next, use a paintbrush dipped in tempera paint and incorporate painting with the glued shapes in various ways:
   - paint around the shapes
   - paint the background paper
   - paint on the shapes
   - paint any combination of these ideas
5. While the paint is still wet, press other torn paper shapes into the wet paint.
6. Allow the painted design with torn collage papers to thoroughly dry.

Picasso 1881-1973

*Early in Picasso's (PIH-**KAH**-SO) career, before he was a famous Cubist, he had a personal style of painting and expressing himself called his Blue Period. He focused on paintings with themes of loneliness, using primarily blue paint to express sad feelings on his canvas.*

One Color Painting

MATERIALS
- tempera paint, one main color
- tempera paint, small amounts of other colors to mix into the main color
- several jars for mixing paints
- paintbrushes
- large jar of clear water for rinsing
- large white paper

PROCESS
1. Select a color as the main color and theme of the painting. For this project, blue will be used as the example but any color can be chosen instead of blue.
2. Pour a little blue paint in several jars. Add just a touch of a different color to each jar to slightly change the blue paint to a new shade. For example, add a little white to the first jar of blue and it becomes powder blue. Add a tiny bit of green to the next jar and it becomes aqua. Add just a smidgen of black to the third jar of blue and it becomes a gray-blue. The main idea is to keep the color blue, but in new shades.
3. When a nice selection of blues has been mixed (remember to keep one jar pure blue), it is time to paint. Paint a picture using shades of blue as the only colors.
4. Dry the painting.

VARIATION
- Think of a theme, an emotion, or a feeling. Think of what colors would express that theme or feeling. Paint in tones and shades of one color that are most expressive for that feeling. For example, a sad painting might be in blue. A happy painting might be in shades of yellow. A painting of anger might be in shades of red. Green might express peace and tranquillity.

Pablo Picasso

Pablo Picasso was the most famous painter of the 1900's, working with sculpture, graphics, ceramics, drawing, and painting. He is most remembered as a Cubist. Before Picasso became a famous Cubist, he had a personal style of painting and expression called his Blue Period (1901-1904) focusing on paintings with themes of loneliness and despair, using primarily blue paint to communicate these themes. He later moved to a style stressing warmer colors and moods called the Rose Period (1904-1906).

Young artists experiment with only one color of paint mixed in different shades just like Picasso did in his Blue Period, perhaps painting with blue like Picasso, or possibly choosing red, yellow or other shades instead.

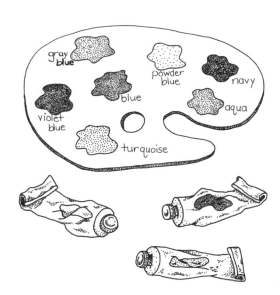

Picasso 1881-1973

Pablo Picasso

Pablo Picasso is one of the most famous artists of all time. He was an artistic genius and is particularly remembered for his style of art called Cubism. Picasso grew up in Spain and later studied and lived in Paris. As a child, Picasso showed incredible artistic talent and was considered a child prodigy. In fact, Picasso's father, who was also an artist, gave all of his own art supplies to 13 year old Picasso because he showed such amazing talent. By the time he was nineteen, Picasso was a fully trained, professional painter. He moved to Paris and lived a very poor, simple life while painting over 200 works. These paintings showed his sadness over what he saw and felt about the poor lives of those around him. This was called his Blue Period. But then, Picasso began to paint a happier type of painting showing clowns and performers at the circus. This was called his Rose Period. Next he began to paint pictures that looked more like puzzles with the pieces all out of order. Sometimes Picasso would stick things to his paintings like newspaper clippings, a bottle label, buttons, cloth, or string - a technique called collage invented by Picasso. Picasso painted until the very day he died at the age of 92 years.

Picasso and the other Cubists tried to create a new way of seeing things in art. They would look at something and try to break it apart in the way they painted it. For instance, Picasso tried to show the models he painted from all sides at once, not just from one normal view. He might show a woman with her eyes facing the right but her nose turned to the left. Her basic body shapes would be changed into cubed or square shapes, facing various directions at once. She might be put together somewhat like a jigsaw puzzle or a broken mirror. Many other artists learned from what Picasso painted and incorporated this into their own sculptures and paintings. Cubism changed the concept of art and led the way to Surrealism and Modern Art.

Young artists explore Picasso's Cubist technique of painting a picture that looks like jumbled puzzle pieces by cutting apart a painting of a friend and then putting it back together Cubist style.

Picasso (PIH-**KAH**-SO) is one of the most famous artists of all time, a child prodigy and genius remembered for his style of art called Cubism, paintings whose outcomes resemble a piece of broken glass.

Fractured Friend

MATERIALS

- white drawing paper (9"x12")
- paints and brushes
- drawing paper, (9"x12"), any color
- some collage items, such as -
  newspaper clippings
  buttons
- dark crayon (optional)
- scissors

  bottle labels
  cloth
- white glue

  string
  paper bits

PROCESS

1. Ask a friend to act as a model for this painting. The friend should sit or stand in an open area near the artist. The artist looks at the model and paints a painting on the white paper. It doesn't have to look exactly like the friend. Paint the way it feels best. Then allow the painting to dry overnight.
   Note: If the painting has curled while drying, it can be ironed by an adult with an iron on a medium setting. First cover the board with clean newsprint. Place the painting on the newsprint. Next place another sheet of paper over the painting. Iron slowing until the curls come out.

2. The painting can be cut apart free-hand with scissors, or lines can first be drawn with a dark crayon and then cut. If drawing lines, mark out some large shapes like puzzle pieces on the painting. Squares, triangles, and other Cubist shapes work well. Cut the painting apart on or near these lines.
   Note: The line can be sketchy instead of solid. The pieces should be bold and not small.

3. Next, glue the pieces of the painting onto the remaining sheet of paper. They can be glued in order or out of order. Upside down pieces work well too. When all the pieces are glued on the paper, glue a few more collage items into the Cubist design to experience Picasso's idea of collage.

4. When satisfied with the art work, it is complete. The friend will be fractured in Cubist shapes with collage items mixed in, just like Picasso would appreciate.

Picasso continued

Katie Rodriquez, age 8, Profile Portrait

Rivera  1886-1957

Diego Rivera

Diego Rivera grew up in Mexico and then lived for awhile in Europe where he studied art. While in Europe, he came under the Cubist influence. Later in Italy, he was deeply impressed by Renaissance frescoes (paintings on wet plaster walls and ceilings). After his return to Mexico, he became world famous for his paintings, especially for his wall murals, showing the everyday lives of Mexican workers and Mexican children.

A mural is a picture painted on a large surface, like the wall of a building, either indoors or out. Rivera would often paint directly on damp plaster, creating a fresco. Many of his murals are extremely large, decorating the walls of important public buildings.

Young artists create gigantic murals with the help of a slide projector and a few friends. This work of art can be a team project!

*Diego Rivera (REE-**VER**-AH) is world famous for his gigantic murals of Mexican life.*

Giant Projector Mural

MATERIALS
- slide projector
- slide with a picture you like
- roll of large paper
- tape
- pencils
- tempera paint and paintbrushes

PROCESS
1. Tape a large piece of paper from the roll onto a wall.
2. Set the slide projector on the floor facing the paper on the wall.
3. Select a slide for the art project such as a that of an animal, a building, or a picture of the young artist. Place it in the slide projector.
4. Darken the room and turn on the projector, shining the slide on the paper.
5. Next, draw around the main shapes in the slide image with a pencil.
   Note: It helps to stand off to one side to draw or to step in front of the projector to block the projector light when checking the lines that were drawn.
6. Outline the main shapes and don't worry about drawing every little detail in the image. Then turn off the projector and finish the pencil drawing.
7. Paint the pencil drawn mural with tempera paints.
8. After the giant mural is dry, trim the edges of the paper and hang it on a wall or even on a ceiling!

Rivera, c. 1945

Duchamp 1887-1968

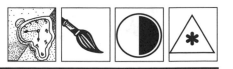

*Duchamp (DOO-**SHAMP**) was an inventive, playful artist who believed in "happy accidents" in his work.*

Happy Accident String Drop

MATERIALS

- pieces of yarn or string about 6"-12" in length
- dishes of tempera paint
- covered work area
- large sheet of paper taped to the floor
- tweezers, optional

PROCESS

1. Cut pieces or string or yarn into any variety of lengths, not exceeding 12".
2. Fill a shallow dish or container with tempera paint, one container for each color.
3. Drape a string into each dish, leaving the end hanging over the edge of the dish as a finger-hold. The rest of the string should be covered and soaking in paint.
4. Place a large sheet of paper on the floor. Tape the corners so the paper stays in place.
5. Pull a strand of string from one of the dishes, wringing out some of the paint against the lip of the dish while pulling.
6. Stand on the floor with the string dangling above the paper on the floor and drop the string, allowing the string to loop or curve naturally in any design as it lands on the paper. For an extra bright design, pat the string with a hand or a paintbrush to force more paint from the string onto the paper.
7. Remove the string with tweezers or fingers. Replace the string in the dish of paint.
8. Continue dropping pieces of paint-soaked string in any variety of colors on the paper, making natural designs. When satisfied with the complete design, remove the paper to a drying area. Dry for several hours.

Marcel Duchamp

Marcel Duchamp was a French painter and the leader of a group of painters who called themselves Dadaists. Dadaists were known as brilliant innovators and freethinkers. They used the term Dada to describe their group, which is the nonsense baby talk word for "hobby horse" in French, a word like "goo-goo" in English. The word, dada, expressed that their art was absurd and they hoped to shock the art community. All of the Dada group enjoyed trying new, wacky, or unusual ideas that had not be tried before.

As Duchamp became a well-known artist, he moved to the United States to show his works. Duchamp was an inventive, playful artist who believed in "happy accidents" in the Dadaist style of art. One of his favorite art techniques was to drop pieces of string on a sheet of paper and then record their curves and designs in various artistic ways and art mediums.

In this rendition of Duchamp's "happy accident", young artists soak string in paint and then drop the string on a large sheet of paper, automatically recording the design in the Dada style.

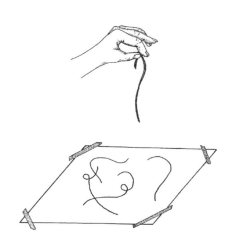

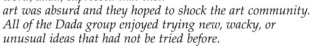

Hans Arp

Hans Arp was a sculptor, graphic artist, painter and writer who lived mostly in Zurich, Switzerland. He designed tapestries and wrote many pieces of poetry and prose in both French and German. As an artist, he was part of the group called Dadaists, and later, a Surrealist.

Hans Arp, like many other Dada artists, believed in the artistic law of chance. He invented a new kind of collage technique where he tore paper into squares and then dropped the pieces through the air from above and watched them land on a larger sheet where they formed a natural design of chance. Hans Arp never knew where the squares would land, but he loved the surprise of watching what happened and gluing them in place as a collage.

Young artists create natural designs experienced by Dadaists like Hans Arp as they explore the "Muse of Chance Collage", also known as the "collage of happy accidents".

Morgan Van Slyke, age 1, Paper Collage

Hans Arp (ARP) invented a new kind of collage technique where paper squares were dropped on a larger sheet of paper. Arp never knew where the squares would land, but he loved the surprise of finding out and gluing them in place.

Muse of Chance Collage

MATERIALS
- torn shapes of heavy, colored construction paper
- larger sheet of paper, any color desired
- white glue or glue stick
- chair, optional

PROCESS
1. Tear pieces of colored construction paper into squares or other shapes.
2. Place the larger sheet of paper on the floor.
3. Stand next to the paper or stand on a chair above the paper and drop one torn piece of paper on the larger one on the floor. If it lands on the paper, use glue to stick it to the larger paper.
4. Drop another piece of torn paper. Glue it where it lands.
5. Continue dropping and gluing paper shapes where they land until satisfied with the collage. It is not necessary to use all the torn shapes.

VARIATIONS
- Experiment with a variety of papers for tearing, such as -

colored art tissue	junk mail	thin cardboard
old playing cards	catalog pages	grocery sacks

- Cut paper into shapes instead of tearing.
- First cover the larger sheet with white glue so the pieces stick as they fall.
- Sprinkle confetti and glitter over a sheet covered with glue.

Oppenheim 1913-1985

*Meret Oppenheim's (**AHP**-EN-HYM) most famous piece of Dada art is a cup, saucer, and spoon covered in real fur.*

Wacky Work of Dada

MATERIALS

- collection of junk
- cardboard
- glue
- paints and brushes
- stapler
- hammer and nails
- marking pens
- scissors

PROCESS

1. Collect and select special junk. Look over the junk and decide how to twist the concept of a piece of junk to make it "not work" or make it opposite its natural use. For example, with an old paint box, fill the paint cups with fur or buttons instead of paint. Or, with an old vase or pot, have it sprout knives, forks, and spoons instead of flowers. Or, with a broken egg beater, decorate the beaters with plastic flowers. With old glasses, decorate the broken lenses with crazy wrapping paper.

2. Once an absurd and wacky idea is in mind, begin assembling and attaching items with hammer and nails, glue, stapler, or whatever will work to hold the assemblage together. The idea may develop as it progresses according to art supplies on hand.

3. Dry if necessary.

4. Think up a name for the Dada assemblage, if desired. For example, the vase filled with knives, forks, and spoons might be called *Mealtime Blossoms* or *Stainless Flower Service for Two*. The old glasses with lenses covered in wrapping paper might be called *Eye See* or *Look at Me*. Of course, these are only suggestions and young artists will think up their own.

VARIATION

- Have an art show for the Dada art. Make name tags for the titles of the works. Paint cardboard boxes in black or white for pedestals to display the assemblages. Invite people to come and see the show and talk about what they see.

Meret Oppenheim

Meret Oppenheim, an American artist, considered herself a member of a group of artists who called themselves Dadaists. This group was made up of zany, charming artists who produced amusing works of art called Dada, a "baby-talk" word like "goo-goo" used by a very small child meaning rocking horse in French. The Dadaists liked the name Dada because it symbolized how simple and amusing and absurd their art could be – a complete change from the art of that present time. Meret Oppenheim, a perfect example of a Dadaist, created her most famous piece of Dada: a cup, saucer, and spoon covered in real fur.

The materials useful in creating a Dadaist object can be anything, especially assorted and collected junk such as scrap paper, feathers, fabric, fake fur, buttons, household furnishings, broken toys, old clocks or kitchen items, machine parts, and so on. To explore the amusing world of Dadaists, the young artist collects and selects junk and throw-aways to create a wacky work of Dada.

Nici Smith, age 11, Cowboy Sculpture

Chagall 1887-1985

Marc Chagall

The Jewish Russian painter, Marc Chagall, was famous for a modern style of art called Fantastic art which is similar to Surrealism in its dream-like quality. It is also a mixture of Cubism and imagination influenced by childhood memories, folklore, and country life. Chagall is probably best known for his paintings based on Jewish folktales and theater scenes painted with bright color and a mixture of fantasy and abstraction. Often his paintings seem like dreams, with a young man looking very much like Chagall to be found in many of the paintings.

Chagall painted great numbers of paintings, large-scale murals, etchings, and wonderful stained glass. Because he loved the theater, ballet, and opera, Chagall often designed the stage sets and painted the scenery for the productions using fantasy and bright colors. In this large-scale theater project, young artists experience Chagall's style as a scenery designer and painter by planning and creating a set for a children's play, and then producing the play for others to enjoy.

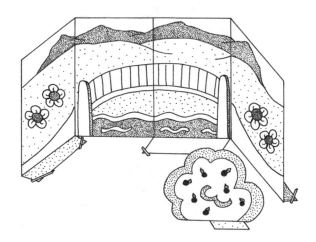

Chagall's (SHAH-GAHL) paintings often seem like dreams, with a young man looking very much like Chagall in many of the paintings.

Scenery Mural

MATERIALS

- large sheets of cardboard from appliance boxes
- razor knife for adult use
- large rolls of shipping tape
- bulletin board paper or craft paper (comes on large rolls)
- black marking pen for sketching out scenery
- tempera paints and brushes
- newspaper to cover floor
- children's play of choice
- costumes of choice
- area to use for a stage

PROCESS

1. Decide on a children's play or story to act out and produce such as a well known story or fable, a favorite children's book or fairy tale, or an original story created by a child. For example:

   The 3 Billy Goats Gruff   Caps for Sale   Rumplestiltskin   Strega Nona

2. Plan out one large mural or scene that will work for the background of most of the play. For instance, in *The Three Billy Goats Gruff*, a woodsy backdrop with leaves and a river would work throughout the entire story. In *Caps for Sale*, a tree or hillside would work well for most of the play. To prepare the backdrop, an adult can score and bend the appliance box cardboard so that it will stand on its own in three sections. Wide shipping tape can be used to help stabilize the cardboard. Tape it to the floor, too, if needed. (See illustration.)

4. Stand the backdrop in the area where the play will take place. Cover the cardboard backdrop with the craft paper, using more tape as needed. Cover both sides if two scenes will be designed. With large arm movements, sketch out the basic design of the backdrop, such as, trees, some leaves, a path, cottage, or whatever is desired. Details can be added later. Just get the basic shapes and outlines sketched out.

6. Line the floor around the cardboard with old newspapers and set up the paints and brushes. Paint the scenery with the tempera paints and brushes. Small details will not show for those watching the play, so use large shapes and bright colors.

7. While the scenery is drying, practice the play over and over. Assemble and wear costumes, if desired. Sometimes props work just as well as full costumes, such as a hat, a cane, a basket, and so on. When ready, perform the play for others.

Magritte 1898-1967

*"Sur" can mean "beyond" in French. Sur-realist artists like Magritte (MAH-**GREE**) created art works that were "beyond reality".*

Giant Tennis Shoes

MATERIALS
- white drawing paper
- pencil and eraser
- watercolor paints and brushes, optional

PROCESS
1. Take off a shoe and set it on the table next to a sheet of drawing paper. Carefully draw a detailed picture of the shoe. Make it as realistic as possible, and big enough to fill the whole sheet of paper. Draw all the seams and stitches, the shoelaces, the texture of the plastic sole and heel.
2. When the shoe drawing is finished, add tiny people and animals to the scene. As suggestions, draw a family living in the shoe, like the nursery rhyme, with doors and windows, a flower bed, a driveway and a new car. Or perhaps the shoe drawing will become a mountain for a team of climbers, or a boat for fishermen sailing on the sea. Use imagination!
3. If desired, paint in the people, animals, and shoe with watercolor paints. Let dry.

VARIATIONS
- Turn an old shoe or boot into a surrealist sculpture by painting it or adding small figures, paper cut outs, or other things to transform it into something new.
- Draw any object and then add smaller people or objects to make the main object look larger. Some suggestions are:
    - draw an apple to fill the paper, and then add little people climbing on the apple like it was a mountain
    - draw a leaf to fill the paper, and then add little spaceships and aliens exploring and investigating it
    - draw a pizza to fill the paper, and then add little ice skater characters twirling and performing through the cheese

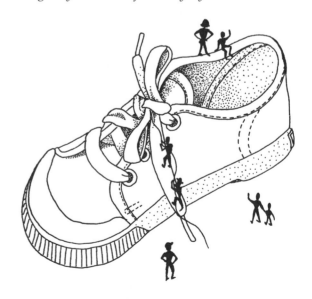

Magritte, c. 1950

Renè Magritte
Renè Magritte lived in Belgium. He led a simple ordinary life, following a schedule that many people would think was fairly dull. However, his artworks show the most remarkable images, such as a painting of a person's eye filled with a cloudy sky, a pair of boots that turn into feet at the toes, and a woman's face patched together as if it were made out of puzzle pieces. Magritte painted everyday objects but turned them into something different, transforming them into magical images that make us stop and think.

One way Magritte and other surrealist painters transformed everyday things was to change the size, making something much bigger or smaller than in the real world. Magritte once painted an apple that was so big it filled an entire room – definitely an apple to notice!

Young artists explore a surrealist technique by creating an imaginary world out of an everyday tennis shoe!

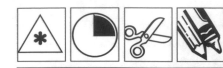

Dali 1904-1985

Salvadore Dali

The group of artists called the Surrealists believed that the unexpected and the unbelievable could happen in art. A clock might melt into a strange, dripping shape. A chair might have the legs of a cat. Stairs could climb yet somehow end beneath themselves. Surrealism is the art of the unreal, where rules such as gravity do not apply and anything can happen.

Salvador Dali, the best known Surrealist, was born in Spain and later lived and created in the United States. He called his surrealist paintings "hand-painted dream photographs" and has amazed others with his outrageous and impossible subjects and ideas. His pictures show strange combinations of objects and figures, often mixing photographs and collage with oil painting. Dali was also a talented jewelry designer, sculptor, and even dabbled in producing motion pictures.

By combining magazine cut-outs with drawing in unexpected ways, young artists can explore the mind set of Surrealists like Salvador Dali. Many children find their way into Surrealism through humor when they first look into the possibilities of the unreal.

Jordan Drost, age 11,
Bovine Ballerina

Salvadore Dali (DAH-LEE) called his surrealist paintings "hand-painted dream photographs", which were filled with outrageous and impossible subjects and ideas.

Dream Photographs

MATERIALS
- large sheet of drawing paper
- colored markers, crayons, colored pencils
- scissors
- glue
- catalogs and magazines for cutting out pictures

PROCESS
1. The adult can pre-select pictures that are clear and uncluttered from magazines or catalogs. Tear them out and save them in a box.
2. Choose a picture with a clear, uncluttered image. Carefully cut it out and glue it on the paper.
3. Next use imagination to draw a picture using the magazine picture in some way that is surprising, unexpected, or impossible. For example, the picture of a bowl of cereal glued to the paper may become the boat upon which a family of hand-drawn or crayon-colored mice sails across a strange ocean. Or, a picture of a woman's face could be used in a drawing as the face of an animal such as a lion, dog, or bear. Cut-outs of coins could be glued on a drawing to represent flowers. The imaginative possibilities are endless and enjoyable.
   Note: More than one cut-out may be used in a drawing.
4. In addition, imagine a title or name for the drawing that is equally unexpected. For example, the coin flowers might be called, *Allowance in Bloom* or *Rich Rewards*. Or, the lion drawing with the woman's face might be titled, *Grizzly Girl* or *My Mom Can Roar*.

VARIATION
- Bright colorful scraps and shapes of paper can also be incorporated into a drawing instead of cut-out magazine pictures (or in addition to the cut-outs).

Giacometti 1901-1966

*Alberto Giacometti (**ZHAK**-O-MEH-TEE) created shocking, strange, surreal sculptures from sticks, paper, wood, wire, and string.*

Sticks 'n Straws

MATERIALS
- any assortment of sticks, such as -
  - toothpicks
  - corn dog skewers
  - bamboo skewers
  - tongue depressors
  - craft sticks
  - dry twigs
  - popsicle sticks
  - coffee stir sticks
- any assortment of straws, such as -
  - drinking straws
  - coffee stir straws
  - bendable straws
- optional materials, such as -
  - wire
  - yarn or floss
  - thin cardboard
- white glue (or, glue-gun with complete adult supervision)
- marking pens, fine point and wide point
- stapler, tape, paper
- matte board or cardboard for base

PROCESS
1. Spread out the assortment of sticks and straws. Think about a scene, building, or sculpture to build. Like Giacometti, a palace is one idea of a sculpture that can be built. Other suggestions are -
   school room   circus tent   child's room   skyscraper   zoo   barn
   scenes from children's books: *Andrew Henry's Meadow, Goodnight Moon,* etc.
2. Using tape, glue, and staplers, begin attaching sticks and straws to the matte board base and build a structure sculpture. If the artist wishes, an adult can use a glue-gun wherever the artist directs to speed up the sculpture process.
3. Cut or draw paper surprises to add to the sculpture, such as Giacometti did when he hung a paper piano keyboard from the ceiling of his palace. The idea is to do something unexpected. Some suggestions are -
   - aquarium in the school room instead of a chalk board
   - mice, fish, and insects in the circus tent instead of animals
   - fancy beds in the barn for the animals to sleep on instead of stalls with hay
4. Think up a name for the sculpture and write it on a card. Attach the card to the sculpture.

Alberto Giacometti
Swiss sculptor Alberto Giacometti created sculptures from sticks, paper, wood, wire, and string that were like drawing with the thin lines of sticks and string. He also had a style of surprising us with ideas and designs that were surreal and apart from everyday reality. This breaking away from reality in art is called Surrealism and can surprise or shock the viewer – just what the Surrealist has in mind. In Giacometti's sculpture, The Palace at 4 AM, *he creates rooms and walls made from thin sticks. But looking closer, he has created a world that is not part of everyday life, with a piano keyboard made from paper hanging from the ceiling.*

Young artists explore the use of sticks and straws to build a sculpture that will surprise others, especially when bits of magazine cutouts or paper drawings are added to the creation to change the reality.

Kahlo 1910-1954

Frida Kahlo

Frida Kahlo grew up in Mexico in the early years of the 20th century. Despite an illness that crippled one of her legs, she had a happy childhood and a loving family. When sixteen years old, Kahlo was in a terrible car accident and almost died. She was plagued by health problems for the rest of her life because of those injuries. As she recovered from the accident, Kahlo began to paint. Many of her paintings are portraits of people in her life and of herself—pictures she painted of her own face. She painted people surrounded by things that were important to them like pets or family and also created many pictures from her childhood and the people in her family.

Young artists draw or paint a self-portrait by looking at their faces in mirrors. A self-portrait will be even more special if it includes special things in the drawing like a favorite shirt or hat, a special toy or doll, a baseball glove, or a model airplane. Whatever objects or possessions mean the most to the artist could be included to make the self-portrait most meaningful. Kahlo is well known for including a pet in many of her paintings, which might be fun to try.

*Kahlo (**CAH**-LO) drew and painted many self portraits of herself from different times in her life, from childhood through adulthood.*

Special Self-Portrait

MATERIALS
- white drawing paper
- pencil and eraser
- choice of coloring tools, such as -
  crayons   markers   colored pencils   paints and brushes
- mirror to look into while drawing
- choice of props to hold or wear and add to drawing, such as -
  hat   toy   pet   uniform

PROCESS
1. Prop a mirror on a table and sit comfortably looking into the mirror, so the reflection of the face can be seen, and draw at the same time. Use as large a mirror as possible, and set it up in a place where there can be plenty of quiet and privacy to work on the drawing.
2. Begin by sketching the face and shoulders lightly. Keep lines that feel right and erase lines that don't. Try to draw what is seen in the mirror, the shape of the mouth and eyes, the way the hair lies next to the face, the shape of the shirt collar.
3. Add special objects that are important to the artist. For example, wear a softball team cap or hold a favorite teddy bear in one arm while drawing. Draw things in the background, too, behind the face like the sunflowers in a special garden or a favorite tree house built with friends. Maybe draw a special pet in the picture too.
4. When the pencil sketch is done, color-in the special self portrait with paint, markers, crayons, or colored pencils. Sign the work with name and date, just like Kahlo did.

Kahlo continued

Geneva Faulkner, age 8, Self-Portrait

Kahlo, Child Self-Portrait, c. 1940

Wright 1867-1959

Frank Lloyd Wright

Frank Lloyd Wright is well known for the uncluttered, clean-cut, strong, and natural architecture he designed, especially homes. Wright believed the interior and exterior of a home should go together as well as suiting the people who would live in the house.

Young artists experiment designing a home by assembling boxes for the rooms and then adding details for exterior and interior design. Just like Frank Lloyd Wright, young architects design their homes to suit their individual styles, likes, and inspirations.

Wright's two most famous designs are the Guggenheim Museum (1960) in New York City, and his own home in Spring Green, Wisconsin.

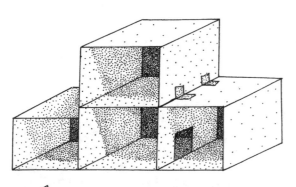

Wright (RITE) believed in uncluttered, clean-cut, strong and natural architecture, both inside the building and out.

Box House Architect

MATERIALS
- cardboard boxes, any shapes and sizes
- scissors
- large sheets of paper to cover boxes, if desired
- heavy paper or construction paper
- scraps for interior design, such as -

wallpaper	carpet	vinyl floor
magazine pictures	fabric	wrapping paper

- masking tape
- knife to cut cardboard, with adult one on one assistance only
- paints and brushes, optional

PROCESS
1. Before beginning the project, an adult can remove flaps from cardboard boxes so the boxes are ready for building.
2. Turn cardboard boxes on their sides, so the opening faces towards the artist like a stage for a play. Choose boxes for the next step.
3. Stack boxes like rooms and join them together with masking tape.
   Note: Most houses are one or two stories, but this creation can be any shape or design desired. Use lots of tape to make the structure strong.
4. An adult can help cut cardboard into shapes or sheets for any of the following:

roof	deck	patio	railing
staircase	steps	balcony	chimney

   Again, assemble with masking tape.
5. The house can be decorated inside with ideas such as the following:
   - carpet and vinyl scraps for floor coverings
   - pictures cut from magazines for wall decor
   - furniture constructed from paper or cardboard
   - fabric scraps attached for draperies or furniture covers
6. The exterior of the house can be painted, covered with paper, sponge-stamped with brick shapes, or left as is. Add landscaping or other outdoor additions made from paper, cardboard, metal pans, pebbles, and so on, such as -

swimming pool or pond	waterfall	gardens	playground or yard

ART TODAY, EVERY WAY

chapter 4

Pop, Op, Folk, Modern, Cartoonists, Photojournalists, & Children's Book Illustrators

Jody Drost, age 9, Winter Barn

Grandma Moses 1860-1961

Anna Mary Robertson

When Anna Mary Robertson was growing up working hard on her family farm, she had no time to paint. She kept on working hard after marrying her husband, Thomas Moses, on the farm they ran together. It was not until Anna Mary was in her eighties and a grandmother that she really found time to paint, and by then, she was called Grandma Moses by family and friends. Her paintings are Folk Art, meaning painted by a person who has no professional training or lessons, and who paints about real life. Grandma Moses' paintings were filled with details of all the happenings and people and pets and horses and trees and buildings and weather in her town. For example, she painted the town square during the Fourth of July celebration showing the entire community in action, all on one canvas. Grandma Moses painted until she was almost 101 when she went into a nursing home and was no longer able to paint.

Young artists draw or paint a busy scene with lots of details on a large sheet of drawing paper.

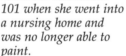

Katherine Shelley, age 8, Asthma Camp

*It was not until Anna Mary Robertson was a grandmother in her eighties that she found time to paint, and by then, she was called Grandma Moses (**GRAND**-MAH **MO**-ZISS) by family and friends, the name she would be known by as a famous artist.*

Busy Folk Art Scene

MATERIALS
- marking pens
- watercolor paints and brushes, optional
- large sheet of drawing paper
- pencil, optional

PROCESS
1. Think of a scene, celebration, or happening with all its details. Think of all the people, places, and things that would be in the scene. For one example, imagine a big birthday party with relatives and friends, gifts, party table, furniture, pets, and maybe even a secret mouse in the corner. Another idea might be to paint a soccer game showing all the players, the field, people watching, trees, birds, and cars parked in the lot nearby. Another idea might be to look at a backyard and draw all the details, such as the swing set, the sidewalk, garden, pets, birds in the trees, and every little bug in the grass.
2. Draw with a pencil first, if desired, or start right in with marking pens.
3. Draw a busy, busy scene with marking pens.
4. Take a rest.
5. Draw some more details in the scene.
6. Rest again.
7. Fill in with watercolor paints, if desired.

Rockwell 1895-1978

*Many of Rockwell's (**RAHK**-WEL) paintings tell a funny story.*

Tell-a-Story Illustration

MATERIALS
- pencil and paper
- drawing paper
- choice of drawing tools, such as -
  colored pencils   crayons   markers   paints and brushes

PROCESS
1. Think about something fun, funny, or enjoyable that happened. For example, remember something that felt really good, like a birthday party, a trip to the beach, or winning a prize at school. Remember something funny that made everyone laugh, like accidentally smearing icing from a cake on your face, falling asleep at the kitchen table, or finding your cat in a strange position on the couch.
   Writing Option: Write a short story about this happy happening or tell the story to an adult helper who will write the words down.
2. Draw a picture to illustrate the story with pencil and then color it any way desired. Choose the best moment of the story and draw a picture that shows what happened. Include details in the drawing. For example, if the story tells about hitting a home run and winning the game, draw the moment of swinging the bat and connecting with the ball. Include the pitcher and the catcher in the drawing, people cheering from the stands, teammates jumping up and down, your baseball cap popping off your head with the effort of hitting the ball.
3. Look carefully at the finished picture. Does the drawing tell the story so well that written words are no longer needed? If so, this is illustrating like the great artist, Norman Rockwell.

Norman Rockwell

Norman Rockwell is known and loved for his humorous paintings of everyday American life. He began his career as an illustrator of children's books in 1916, but soon went to work for the Saturday Evening Post, *a popular magazine of his time. Rockwell painted more than 300 pictures for the cover of this magazine, and his work became a favorite in many households.*

One famous Rockwell picture shows a zookeeper calmly reading a newspaper and eating a sandwich while a hungry lion gazes at the food, inches away behind the bars of its cage. Another shows a young boy in a doctor's office, carefully examining the framed medical school diploma on the wall as if to be sure his doctor is really qualified to give him a shot.

The young artist illustrates drawings or paintings with humor too. The picture can illustrate or tell a funny story without using any words at all.

Hannah Kohl, age 6, Queen & Pig with Wagon

O'Keeffe 1887-1986

Georgia O'Keeffe

As a young girl, Georgia O'Keefe knew she wanted to be a painter and studied painting from then on, even when teachers discouraged her and tried to change her style. She chose to move to New York City to study where she could receive some serious training and attention to her unique talent. She did become a great painter, living late into her 90's and continuing as an artist throughout her lifetime.

Georgia O'Keeffe is famous for her paintings of flowers that fill the canvas, edges of the flower designs often going right off the paper. Sometimes she would paint only a part of a flower on the canvas, that part so close up that you would feel like you were deep inside the flower. O'Keeffe is a totally original American painter uninfluenced by artists from Europe. She found inspiration from nature - from flowers, drift wood, and animal skulls in the desert.

Young artists explore painting a close-up of a flower just like Georgia O'Keeffe.

*Georgia O'Keeffe (O-**KEEF**) is most famous for her paintings of flowers that fill the canvas, blossom edges disappearing right off the paper.*

Close-Up Flower Painting

MATERIALS
- small squares of posterboard
- tempera paints or watercolors
- paintbrushes
- pencil, optional
- cups, cans, dishes, or a large plate for mixing paint colors
- magazine pictures of flowers
- large square of posterboard
- jar of water to clean brushes, rags
- fresh flowers in a vase

PROCESS
1. Set up a work area with paints, brushes, and mixing cups. Have a jar of water for thinning paints and rinsing brushes handy. Rags will help with drying brushes.
2. Place a vase of fresh flowers on the table, or cut out magazine pictures of flowers and tape them to the table.
3. Place a small square of posterboard on the table. This will be a practice painting before doing the larger posterboard.
4. Look at a fresh flower (or a magazine picture of a flower) closely. Use a pencil to lightly sketch the shape of the flower on the posterboard. Allow the edges of the flower sketch to go off the edges of the paper so the flower looks very large and close-up.
5. To practice, paint the flower with the real colors as they exist, or make up new color choices.
6. For the real painting, paint the same flower or another flower or on the very large square of posterboard. When complete, set aside to dry.

VARIATION
- Paint a collection of flowers, a different kind on each square of posterboard.

Nici Smith, age 11, Watercolor Flower

Wyeth 1917-

Wyeth's (WY-ETH) paintings are simple and realistic, detailed and natural.

First Snow

MATERIALS
- white watercolor paper or heavy white drawing paper
- jar of rubber cement glue (Tri-Tex™ is non-toxic)
- pencil and eraser
- newspaper covered work area
- old toothbrush
- watercolor paints and brushes

PROCESS
1. Sketch a simple outdoors scene on a sheet of white watercolor paper or heavy drawing paper. Sketch the scene very lightly with pencil.
   Consider drawing a scene with subjects like those in Wyeth's paintings, such as -
   - old shed in a barren field
   - seashell by a rock at the beach
   - fencepost with dried weeds around the base
   - wild bird perched on a leafless, dry branch
2. Next place the drawing on newspapers. Dip the old toothbrush into the rubber cement. Then drag a thumb across the bristles, splattering tiny drops of rubbery glue onto the white paper. Keep splattering until the sheet of paper is covered with tiny droplets and dots of glue. Let the glue drops dry completely on the paper.
3. Next, paint a picture right on top of the dry glue drops. Simply ignore them! Paint the picture with rich autumn-tone watercolors like Wyeth would use, such as the following suggestions -
   - tans and browns
   - orange autumn leaves
   - blacks and golds
   - dark green pine trees
   - gray sky with storm clouds
4. After the watercolor painting is finished and completely dry, rub away the spots of rubber cement glue with fingers. A perfect white dot of "un-painted paper" should be left beneath each dot of dry glue. When all the glue drops are rubbed away, the watercolor painting will be filled with the appearance of a sparkling white flurry of fresh falling snow, the first snowfall of the year on a late autumn day!

Andrew Wyeth
Andrew Wyeth is one of the most famous American artists of this century. He was raised in a family dedicated to art. Wyeth's father was a famous painter and illustrator of children's books. His brothers and sisters became artists, engineers, and musicians. And a generation later, Andrew's own son, Jamie, has become an important artist. You could say that art runs in the family!

Wyeth is best known for his realistic paintings of the farming country in Pennsylvania where he was raised, and the rocky seacoast of Maine, where he often lives. Many of his paintings are of very simple scenes like a dog in a field of grass, a lace curtain blowing in the breeze, a tiny wildflower in the forest, or an old farm building. Wyeth's paintings are very natural and detailed, often in watercolor and tempera paint.

Young artists can explore one of Wyeth's art techniques that will look like the first, crisp snowfall on a late autumn day in the country.

Jodi Drost, age 9, Winter Barn

Dorthea Lange

Dorthea Lange was an American photographer who recorded history and important events with her camera. In one of Lange's most famous photographs, Migrant Mother, she shows how the failure of crops due to dust storms and droughts affected the farmers of California. Migrant Mother shows a tired migrant worker woman holding her starving children. Many people in America were so moved by Lange's photograph that they helped the people in the drought stricken areas of California and saved many lives. Lange's photographs had the power to get people moving to make changes in the world by telling an important story.

Young photographers tell a story about a real-life event with photos in Photo Story Collage.

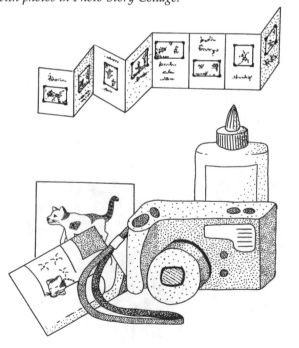

Dorthea Lange (LANG) was an American photographer who recorded history and important events with her camera.

Photo Story Collage

MATERIALS
- instamatic camera with film (or any camera of choice)
- photos developed from the film (several days may be necessary to complete this project with time for developing film included)
- scissors
- glue
- heavy matte boards, one for each photo
- marking pens

PROCESS
1. Look around at people, pets, the neighborhood, the school yard, or the classroom. Notice an event or something happening. Take a picture with the camera of that event. It doesn't have to be anything very unusual. Real-life common events work well for this project. For instance, take a picture of a friend painting at the easel.
2. Next, take another picture that shows what happens next. For instance, take a picture of the friend as she carries her painting to a drying area. Take another picture that shows what happens next. Then another. Then another. Take as many pictures as needed to show a sequence of happenings that tell a story. At least three pictures will be needed, or as many as twelve.
   Note: At this point, if there is film left in the camera, think of another event to photograph in a sequence of happenings. For instance, photograph a cat walking through the room, another photo of it climbing up on the chair, another of it curling into a ball, and another of it falling asleep.
3. An adult can take the film in for developing. (One-hour or overnight developing services work well for young children.)
4. When the photos are developed, spread them out on the table. Sort them by story groups. Choose one story group. Line up the photos in order of the happenings of that story. Glue each photo on a matte. Glue them as they are, or cut them into shapes. Add designs with marking pens to the matte around the photos.
5. Tape the mattes together in order like an accordian. Look at the finished sequence and tell the story of the event shown by the photographs.

Bourke-White 1906-1971

*When Margaret Bourke-White (**BORK**-WITE) was a child she wanted to be a photographer like her father and would pretend to take pictures with an empty box.*

ABC Photography

MATERIALS
- camera
- scissors
- glue stick
- color print film and developing
- matte board or smooth cardboard

PROCESS
1. Start by taking a walk on a sunny afternoon. Bring along a camera loaded with color film and an adult to help with the camera. The assignment is to find, and photograph, every letter in the name of the artist with the camera! Notice letters are everywhere: on stores, on trucks, on billboards and signs. Letters about 6" to 12" tall are easiest to photograph, especially if they're at eye-level and not way up high on a building. Find letters in bright sunlight without any shadows.
2. When looking through the viewfinder on the camera, try to frame the object for the picture so each letter is as big as it can be. Remember - Be Safe: Don't walk out in the street to get a photo, and don't step backwards off a curb while looking through the camera!
3. Take at least two photos of every letter in the name, just in case some of the pictures don't turn out. Have a friend take a photo of the artist, too, if enough film is left after the alphabet letter hunt.
4. When the film is turned in for developing, it might pay to request a double set of prints so there will be twice as many photos for making name plaques. Some of the photos may be fuzzy, but with luck, there will be at least one good picture of every letter in the name of the artist.
5. Glue the photos to a sturdy piece of cardboard or stiff paper to make a hanging name plaque. Use the photos just as they are, or cut them smaller.
6. Tie a piece of yarn on the sides so the name plaque can hang on a nail, or tack it up like a poster.
7. For optional decorations, add lace, glitter, confetti, or other collage items as desired.

Margaret Bourke-White

Margaret Bourke-White always wanted to be a photographer. Her father's hobby was photography. As a little child, she pretended to take pictures with an empty box. As Margaret grew older, her father taught her how to develop film and use real cameras. She began her professional career in college, taking pictures of buildings like houses, skyscrapers and steel mills. She became one of the first photographers for Time Magazine *in 1929, and her adventures with news photography took her all over the world.*

Photography allows a new way to look at things. When pictures are snapped with a camera, details never before noticed are suddenly important. An old building suddenly looks interesting, with its broken windows and unpainted wood. A wooden fence becomes the perfect background for a photo of wildflowers. Sunlight and the shadows can affect how the photograph will turn out.

Young artists take pictures like Bourke-White, but with a special project in mind – ABC Photography.

Ryan Phillips, age 12,
Name Plaque

Lawrence 1917-

Jacob Lawrence

Jacob Lawrence grew up in New Jersey and Pennsylvania during the 1920's and 1930's. After taking an after-school arts and crafts class as a teenager, he decided to become a painter.

During the Great Depression of the 1930's, many Americans were very poor. Lawrence worked for a government program called the WPA during a time often called the Harlem Renaissance. The WPA helped many musicians, writers, and artists get jobs and a jump-start in their work. In 1941 at age 24, Lawrence became the first black American artist to have a painting included in the permanent collection of the Museum of Modern Art, a famous New York museum.

When artists make many pictures about the same subject, it is called a series. Jacob Lawrence created a famous series of paintings during the 1970's that he calls "The Builders". These paintings show people at work, especially carpenters and people who build things out of wood.

Young artists paint or draw a series of pictures about people in their own lives who work.

Lawrence (LOR-ENS) decided to become a painter when he was a teenager after taking an afterschool arts and crafts class.

Series Drawing

MATERIALS
- drawing paper
- pencils, crayons or markers
- paints and brushes, optional

PROCESS
1. Make a series of pictures by yourself or work with friends or classmates to create a series. A topic in the spirit of Lawrence's "builders" series would be "people at work." Think of different ways to illustrate this topic through drawing:
   - people who work at school like teachers, office staff, custodians and students
   - people who work at home, like family members cooking, fixing the car, caring for babies, mowing the lawn
   - people who work in the neighborhood like storekeepers, repair crews, policemen
   - visit the place where mom and dad work and draw the people working there
2. Decide before beginning the series of drawings what common features the series will have. Here are some examples of common features:
   - every picture could be a marking pen drawing, or a watercolor painting, or a tempera painting
   - the use of paper that is the same size for every picture
   - the worker can be drawn using a different tool in every picture
3. Begin drawing the series of pictures. Drawing a series can take many days to complete. Lawrence has worked on his builders series for over 20 years!
4. When finished drawing the series, display all the pictures in a show at school or on a wall at home. Give each of the pictures a series name, such as "Worker #6 - The Mailman", or "Mom Works Very Hard". Write the series name on each drawing and number each one, if desired, just like Lawrence.

Smith 1906-1965

Metal sculptor David Smith (SMITH) once said: "If it's out in the barn, weld it together!"

Cubi Structure

MATERIALS
- wood scraps, small blocks, and cylinders of wood framing scraps
- white glue (electric craft glue-gun with one-on-one adult supervision)
- cardboard square or flat piece of wood for base
- paints and brushes, optional
- masking tape

PROCESS
1. Collect wood scraps from a wood shop class or a picture frame shop. (Rough cut scraps and blocks come in net bags of 10 pounds or more at a reasonable price from school supply stores and catalogs.)
2. Glue a cylinder or rectangle to the base to form a standing post as the central support of the structure. Dry briefly to set.
3. Glue more blocks or cylinders to the post, standing them on edge, balancing, or building and gluing in any style suitable to the artist. (An adult assisted glue-gun gives a solid and speedy structure.)
4. If necessary, add masking tape to temporarily hold the sculpture in place until it dries completely. Remove any masking tape.
5. If desired, paint the Cubi sculpture with tempera or watercolor paints.

VARIATIONS
- Glue and assemble any shapes of wood scraps in any way using glue and tape.
- Build a large outdoor Cubi sculpture like David Smith created from steel, but use cardboard boxes and masking tape or mailing tape.

David Smith

American sculptor David Smith is considered a pioneer in the field of metal sculpture and monumental geometric construction. He is well known for a series of sculptures called Primary Structure in his Cubi series — three large structures of cubes of welded steel stacked high against the sky on single cylinders of steel.

Young artists experience a smaller version of the steel Cubi series sculpture technique by gluing wood block scraps on a cylinder or rectangle block base. The possibilities for design are endless.

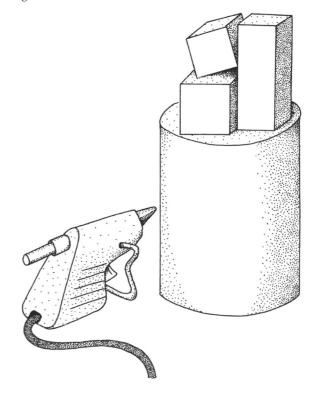

Vasarély 1908-

Victor Vasarély

Vasarély was born in Hungary in 1908 and later moved to Paris to be a part of the group of Op Art and Surrealist artists studying and working there. He is well known for his stark black and white checkerboard designs that are optical illusions, or optical art (Op Art). An optical illusion such as Vasarély's black and white checkerboard design feels like the design is shifting and moving under the eye. (See checkered icon above.) Young artists experiment with Vasarély's crazy checkerboard technique using black marking pens or paint on a white paper background.

Vasarely's (VAH-SAH-RAY-LEE) Op Art checkerboard designs appear to shift, vibrate, and move even though they are completely still.

Dizzy Op Art

MATERIALS
- white paper, 9"x12"
- pencil
- ruler
- black marking pen
- black tempera paint
- glue
- larger sheet of black paper for a frame

PROCESS
1. Place the paper on the work table so that it is like a place mat. With a ruler and pencil, draw about 4 to 6 straight lines from top to bottom. They can be evenly spaced or spaced at different widths. (See the wavy checkered icon above.)
2. Now turn the paper the tall way. Start at the top of the paper and draw one long line – straight, wiggly, or wavy – crossing through the ruled lines and stopping at the bottom edge.
3. Leave a wide space or a narrow space between lines and draw another line next to this, following the first line, or trying a different wiggle or wave. Then leave another space and draw another line. Draw lines from top to bottom, crossing over the ruled lines, until the paper is full.
4. Next, color in every other square – like a checkerboard – with the black marking pen. (Or, paint in every other square with black paint and a paintbrush.) The squares will be all different shapes and not really square. When every other space is filled, the Op Art optical illusion will be complete.
5. Glue the design on a larger sheet of black paper, if desired, to show off the illusion.

VARIATIONS
- Weave straight strips of colored paper through the paper mat which is first cut with wiggly cuts. (See illustration to the left.) Use two contrasting colors instead of black and white, such as purple and yellow, red and green, blue and orange.
- Computer Op Art: In a word processing program, draw curved and straight lines that cross each other. Some areas can be filled and others left white. Print it out.

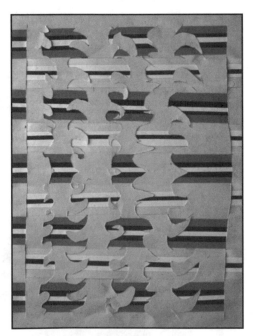

Amanda Schwittay, age 7, Woven Mat

Pollock 1912-1956

*Jackson Pollock (**PAH**-LUHK) wanted his paintings to be different from photography. He created "action painting" which included throwing and spattering paint.*

Action Spatter

MATERIALS
- newspaper covered work area (and masking tape)
- cardboard box with one side cut away (see illustration)
- old clothes or coveralls
- variety of larger brushes
- large containers of tempera paint
- large craft paper or newsprint

PROCESS
1. Cover the work area floor with lots of newspaper. Tape the paper so the sheets stay in place. Place the box on the newspaper, with the opening facing the artist.
   Note: Working outside on the grass or a playground makes for easy clean up too.
2. Place a sheet of craft paper inside the box. Tape if necessary.
3. Cover the artist with old clothing or coveralls to allow for freedom from concern about ruining good clothing.
4. Begin by dipping a large brush into a container of tempera paint.
5. Hold the brush inside the box and splatter the paint onto the paper by shaking the brush from up to down in one large motion. Small motions are messier, but with some control, are also effective.
6. Add more colors and more spattering.
7. Paintings take extra time to dry if spattering is very think.

Jackson Pollock
The American painter Jackson Pollock is known for his experimentation in painting techniques and his abstract style. Pollock wanted his paintings to be different from photography and tried painting what he called "action painting" with his entire body involved in the motion.

Pollock placed his canvas on the ground and then moved rapidly around the picture throwing and spattering paint directly from the paint can onto the canvas. He also used a stick to fling paint from the can onto the emerging interwoven wild design. Sometimes he would add other surprise elements into his action paintings like his own handprints or pieces of his personal possessions. All of his unusual experimentations in painting demonstrate the variety of shape, line, and color that can be found in abstract painting. He once said, "When I am in my painting, I'm not aware of what I'm doing. I have no fears of destroying the image because the painting has a life of its own."

Pollock's style is easily imitated by young artists as they spatter paint from large brushes onto paper. Did Pollock first discover his spattering technique while watching young children?

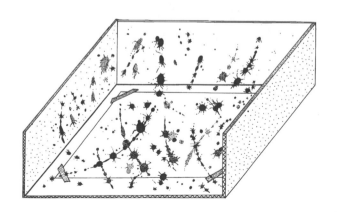

Cornell 1903-1972

Joseph Cornell

A box collage is a three-dimensional construction built in a shallow box. The box hangs on the wall, holding the collage and framing it. American sculptor, Joseph Cornell, was famous for creating box collages. His works look very mysterious, as if there are secret messages hidden in each design. Cornell loved to collect things to put in his box art, especially precious objects and small things of great beauty. Cornell was not trained as an artist but became one of the most famous sculptors of his time.

Each young artist creates a box collage that tells about who the artist is - a self-portrait collage. Think about things that are special, like a favorite color, special souvenirs, collections, or something created. The artist could cut out magazine photos that show things the artist likes to do now or hopes to do someday. Include a scrap of a favorite pair of outgrown jeans, a little toy from the artist's past, or a lock of the artist's hair. The young artist makes a collection of collage elements that express the artist's special personality.

Jacob Aiello, age 8, Baseball Box

Cornell (COR-*NEL*) loved to collect things to put in his box constructions, especially precious objects and small things of great beauty.

Portrait Box Collage

MATERIALS
- special, personal collected collage items
- cardboard box or box lid, about 9"x12" with 2"-3" high sides
- scissors
- white glue
- tempera paint and paintbrush
- colored marker pens
- newspaper covered work area

PROCESS
1. An hour or two before beginning, paint the box a solid color, like white or black, inside and out. Let it dry completely.
2. Spread the collection of collage elements out on the worktable. Think about how the items can be arranged inside the box. Use all of the collected items or only a few.
3. To build the box collage, follow any of these ideas:
   - **Glue things** to the back and sides of the box.
   - **Draw, paint, or color** on the back and sides of the box.
   - **Hang things** from the top of the box with string or yarn.
   - **Poke holes** in the sides and stick things across the box.
   - **Glue things** to little chunks of wood or foam and attach them to the back of the box so they stick out.
   - **Set things** on the bottom of the box.
4. Tape a piece of clear plastic over the front of the box to make it look more like a framed work of art. When finished, hang the box collage on the wall or stand it on a shelf.

Nevelson 1900-1988

*Nevelson (**NEH-VUL-SUN**) is famous for her "art-in-a-box". She is remembered as being a child who saved scraps of wood for art.*

Scrap Box Art

MATERIALS
- wood scraps
- other wooden items, such as -

beads	clothespins
drawer pulls	drawer handles
framing scraps	curtain rings

- saved or collected scraps, such as -

machine parts and pieces	paper plates
buttons	bits and pieces of cardboard
packing materials	dowel or rod pieces

- glue (glue-gun with one-on-one adult assistance)
- one color of paint and paintbrush
- small bottle or can of gold paint and small paintbrush
- newspaper covered work area

PROCESS
1. Assemble the collected scraps and pieces on the newspaper covered work area. Look them over and notice shapes and sizes. Pull out some favorites with which to begin the project.
2. Place the wooden box or crate on the work area. Begin gluing wood scraps and other items into the box.
3. Fill the box in any way desired. Any design or assemblage is acceptable.
4. When the box is filled as desired, paint the entire box and all its contents with a single color of paint. Dry overnight.
5. When dry, touch bits of gold paint here and there to highlight the shapes and textures in the assemblage, if desired. Dry again and display on a wall or in a shelf.

Louise Nevelson
Louise Nevelson was born in Russia around 1900, but grew up in Maine. When she was a child, Nevelson's father owned a lumberyard and she had access to wonderful scraps of wood. She used to nail or glue woodscraps onto other wood pieces and make "assemblages", or art created from odds, ends, scraps, and junk. It wasn't until late in Nevelson's career that she moved on from painting and began creating her wood scrap assemblages in earnest. She became famous for her unique kind of sculpture.

The young artist creates a Nevelson assemblage by gluing scraps and other materials into a cardboard or wooden box. The sides of the box will frame the sculpture. Coating it with one color of paint gives the shapes a texture that brings out the design of the assemblage and disguises the parts and pieces.

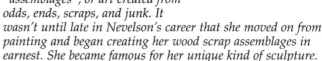

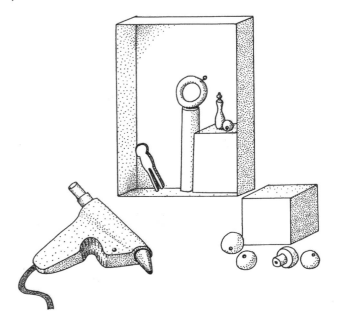

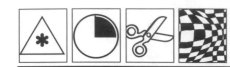

Rauschenberg 1925-

Robert Rauschenberg

Robert Rauschenberg became interested in art when he was in the US Navy in 1942. While visiting a museum, the works of art he saw there sparked his own artistic talent. He then studied painting in 1948 and began a series of works done all in black and white. Later he became interested in creating art with common objects, and explored collage (flat pictures made with many pasted together images) and assemblage (three dimensional pictures with objects that stick out). Rauschenberg included many different things in his works called "combines": soda pop bottles, stuffed chickens, kitchen tools, neckties, snapshots, radios, and signs.

Young artists create a combine from collected pictures and small objects that go together within a theme or subject, for example, "Things I Like Best", "All About Football", or "My Grandpa". The collection is glued together to make a combine in the style of Rauschenberg.

Morgan Van Slyke, age 1, with mom, Becky Van Slyke

*Rauschenberg (**RAW**-SHIN-BERG) included wonderful, imaginative objects and materials in his "combines": soda pop bottles, stuffed chickens, kitchen tools, neckties, snapshots, radios and signs.*

Combines

MATERIALS
- a collection of pictures and small objects
- a sturdy sheet of cardboard or matte board
- a low-temperature electric glue gun, one-on-one adult supervision
- paints and brushes

PROCESS
1. Choose a theme. Spend several days assembling the collection and gathering pictures and objects that fit the subject. Choose from saved snapshots, pictures cut from magazines, lables from cans and boxes, postage stamps, child made drawings and sketches, dried flowers and weeds, and any small objects that can be glued on the collection cardboard.
2. Spread the collection out on a work table. Play around with arranging materials into an interesting pattern or design.The gluing step is next.
3. First plan what things will glue underneath, and what things will glue on top. Work from the bottom up, gluing the back layers first. Cover the entire surface of the cardboard with images, objects, or areas painted with different colors. Dry.
4. Write the title of the work (the subject or theme of the collection) on the back of the cardboard. Display the work. Others may guess the name of the collection, and if it is easy to guess, a good job of expressing an idea with images has been accomplished.

VARIATION
- Clear "Con-Tactô"™ plastic can capture a magazine illustration. To do this, place a piece of the adhesive plastic on top of a magazine picture. Rub hard with fingers to press the plastic very firmly onto the magazine picture. Place the stuck-together plastic and picture in a pan of warm water and soak for several minutes. Next, gently rub the paper away from the back of the plastic. If the magazine has good "coated" paper, it will rub away completely leaving a transparent image of the photograph stuck to the clear plastic like a stained glass window. Use these see-through pictures in a "combine."

Chamberlain 1927-

*Chamberlain (**CHAM**-BER-LIN) creates with metal junk, fragments of old machinery, parts of wrecked cars, and collected parts and pieces from the junk yard.*

BIG Junk

MATERIALS
- strong cardboard box or crate
- collected junk and car parts
- wrench, screw driver, pliers, wire brush
- sheet of plywood, about 3/4" thick, any size desired
- grease cleaner (citrus based and non-toxic) , in a bucket with wire brushes
- Fixall™ plaster compound (non-toxic) from a hardware or building supply store
- materials to attach junk to wood, such as -
  - hammer   nails   wire   screws   screw driver   big stapler

- soap, water, rags
- sheets of newspaper
- latex gloves to protect hands

PROCESS
1. Visit a junk yard or a car recycling business. Ask permission to go through parts and discards. Collect select parts in a cardboard box, and take them home.

2. Fill a bucket with non-toxic citrus based grease cleaner. Dip the parts in the bucket and scrub them with a wire brush until all the grease is gone. Use the wrench, screw driver, and pliers to disassemble parts. They can be left apart or reassembled for the relief sculpture. Wear latex gloves for protection. This is a messy job! When all the parts are clean, wash up with soap and water. Dry the parts outside in the sun or inside on thick sheets of newspaper.

4. When parts are dry, mix Fixall™ according to the directions on the box. Spread Fixall™ on the plywood and press a car part into the stuff to hold. (If necessary, use a hammer and nails, or a screwdriver and screws, to attach the parts to the wood instead of the Fixall™. Wire may also be effective.) Fixall™ dries quickly and rock hard, so spread small amounts in the working area on the plywood rather than covering the entire sheet of plywood. Attach the junk and parts in either a planned or random design.

5. Add more parts and junk until the entire sheet of plywood is covered. Dry for several days. Lean the relief against a wall or fence to display. Or, attach a heavy wire to the back through screw-in hooks, and display on a wall from solid nails.

John Chamberlain

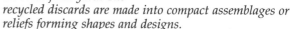

Modern sculpture of today can be very exciting to look at and to build. One new and different artistic expression is accomplished with metal junk, fragments of old machinery, parts of wrecked cars, and collected parts and pieces from the local junk yard. The recycled discards are made into compact assemblages or reliefs forming shapes and designs.

John Chamberlain, a modern American junk artist, collected car parts. Then he made a relief by sticking them to a heavy board and forming the junk into the shapes of flowers with petals.

Young artists explore the Chamberlain technique of collecting big junk and creating a relief on a heavy piece of plywood. This is an adventurous, time consuming project.

Kienholz 1927-

Edward Kienholz

Kienholz is an American Pop Art assemblage artist – a sculptor who builds and constructs environments from ready-made objects and the addition of his own selected materials. His art has been called "Funk Art Tableau". Kienholz's assemblages always have a theme or a message to shock or make the viewer think. The large as life size of the sculptures he creates make them more powerful and noticeable than if they were miniature.

To explore the life-size art assemblage technique of Kienholz, the young sculptor must build with actual life-sized objects and materials, constructing an environment or scene that may invite viewers to walk through, look, and touch. For example, a wall, window, and door built to life size and constructed from cardboard and tape could be a Pop Art environment. Features added such as window shades or curtains, a door knob, and perhaps a cat peeking out the window would add to the reality of the environment. To imitate Kienholz, make the sculpture look as real as possible.

The large as life size of the sculptures Kienholz (KINE-HOLZ) creates make them more powerful and noticeable than if they were tiny or miniature.

Walk Through Sculpture

MATERIALS

- life sized collected materials of choice to fit the theme of the environment assemblage
- cardboard boxes
- sheets of cardboard
- light weight wood scraps
- large colored craft paper from rolls
- rolled tubes of newspaper, taped to hold
- any additional materials of choice
- glue-gun optional (with complete adult supervision)
- knife for cardboard (supervised only)
- drawing paper
- paint and paintbrushes
- tape, glue, stapler

PROCESS

1. Decide on a theme or life-size environment for the Walk Through Sculpture. Think of a scene that would be especially interesting to share with others walking through, touching, and looking. Some ideas might be:
   a castle   an art studio   a space ship   a dungeon   a prehistoric cave
2. Begin building the environment. Cardboard boxes or large pieces of cardboard are most effective for quick walls and basic structure.
3. With complete adult supervision, cut windows or doors or other design features from the cardboard. Adult help will also be required if a glue-gun is used.
4. Add other details to the sculpture with paint and miscellaneous materials of choice.
5. Work until satisfied with the sculpture. It may take a long time to build this environment, often two or more days.
6. Think up a name for the sculpture. Write it on a piece of paper or cardboard and attach it to the work in some way. When the assemblage is ready for viewing, invite others to come and walk through the life-sized Pop Art environment.

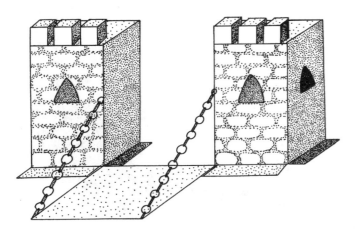

Christo 1935-

*Christo (**KREE**-STO) once built an orange cloth curtain 1/4 mile long to cover a valley in Colorado. Another time he wrapped an entire bridge in Paris with cloth. Once he built floating pink plastic skirts to surround eleven islands in Florida.*

Transformations

MATERIALS

Objects from nature or everyday objects or junk:

- piece of wood
- bicycle
- teapot
- rock
- small fir tree
- old book
- shell
- lawnmower
- kitchen appliance
- autumn leaves
- mailbox
- tool

Supplies and materials to help transform the object into something new:

- rope
- feathers
- surveyor's plastic ribbon
- fabric
- foil
- paints & brushes
- duct tape
- garbage bags
- glue
- toilet paper
- cardboard

PROCESS

1. Select an object to transform. Plan a way to change the object so it will look completely new (transformed), but in a way that people can still recognize its original form. Here are a few suggestions for ways to do this:

   - **Paint** "the object" a new color; for example, paint a bunch of autumn leaves bright pink and purple, then lay them carefully in a row in the yard. Push a bamboo skewer through each leaf into the ground so they will not blow away. They will still look like leaves, but completely transformed leaves which will make people stop and stare!

   - **Wrap** "the object" with thin fabric and tie it tightly with string. The original shape of the object will show through the wrapping, but it will be transformed by the covering. For instance, wrap a teapot with thin fabric and tie it with string. Does it still look like a teapot? (See illustration.)

   - **Glue** a new and unusual surface onto "the object", like feathers on a teacup, fur all over an old shoe, or a banana tightly wrapped with shiny aluminum foil.

   - **Attach** something to "the object" that does not belong, like wings on a radio, a light switch glued to a computer disk, or a garbage bag over a mailbox (with a hole cut to deliver the mail).

2. Display the object where others will notice and enjoy it.

Javacheff Christo

Christo, a highly innovative and imaginative artist, grew up in Bulgaria and later moved to the United States. Christo became famous for huge outdoor art projects which temporarily transform normal places into visually imaginary landscapes. For example, he once created an orange cloth curtain 1/4 mile long to cover an entire valley in Colorado. Another time he wrapped a bridge in Paris with fabric. Once he built floating pink plastic skirts to surround eleven islands in Florida.

Christo spends many years planning and engineering his projects, and requires the help of hundreds of people to assemble and create them. The projects are usually in place for only a few days while many photographs are taken to document and record the artwork. Thousands of people come to see Christo's works, and many more look at the amazing photographs. He helps people see the world in new ways.

Young artists challenge their imaginations like Christo by transforming an everyday object into something new.

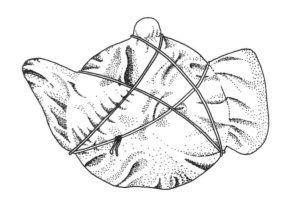

Paik 1932-

Nam June Paik

Nam June Paik was born in Korea, grew up in Japan, studied video art in Germany, and eventually lived in New York City. He built his first robot contraption in 1964 called "Robot K-456", a remote control art machine that could walk, talk, and perform. Nam June Paik is a contemporary sculptor who uses television sets to build robot people. Paik has made whole families of robot people or TV sculptures with grandparents, aunts and uncles, parents and kids. Many TV's in Paik's sculptures are electronically wired together to play videos that Paik makes himself.

For an easy project, the young artist invents a robot design on paper using a pile of old tool and appliance catalogs. For a more challenging video art project, the artist builds a robot including a videotape of a real person's face to be used as the robot's head in the sculpture.

*Nam June Paik (NAHM JUN **PAY**) built a robot contraption in 1964 called "Robot K-456", a remote control art machine that could walk, talk, and perform.*

Robot People

MATERIALS
Easy Paper Robot –
- old catalogs to cut up (especially tool, computer, and appliance catalogs)
- white drawing paper
- scissors
- glue

Challenging Video Robot –
- materials to decorate the cardboard shape of the robot, such as -

paints and brushes	colored paper
shiny wrapping paper	foil
ribbon	buttons
beads	plastics
cellophane	scraps of wallpaper
scraps of carpet	parts of broken toys & machines
general collage and junk collection	

- large sheets of cardboard
- glue and tape, stapler
- working TV and VCR
- blank video tape
- knife to cut cardboard, adult only
- camcorder

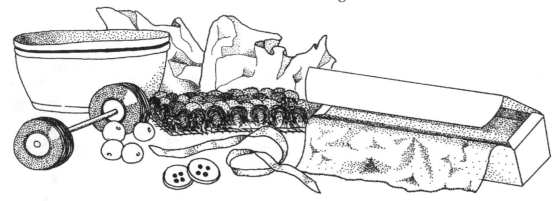

Paik continued

PROCESS

Easy Paper Robot –

1. Look through catalogs to find just the right pages of tools, hardware, or appliances for the robot design. Tear out those pages to save. Set the catalogs aside when done.

2. Cut parts for the robot creation from the torn pages that were saved. Use anything that is part of a tool or a machine. Cut carefully right along the edge of the picture.

3. Glue the cut-out parts together on paper to "build" a robot. For example, a TV might be the head of a robot, buttons from a telephone might be the chest of the robot, and perhaps some portable stereo radios might be the legs. There is no right or wrong way to put together these crazy robots! (See the example to the right.)

4. Glue on lots of little robot details, like dials and digital read-outs, control panels, switches, antenna, wires and cords.

5. Give the robot a name and think about its abilities. What can it do? What does it do best of all? Does it talk? How would it move? What trouble can it get into?

Challenging Video Robot -

1. With adult help, video tape the head and face of someone so their face fills the screen. This face action will be the head of the robot when the tape is played in the VCR and TV. The person being taped should makes faces, pretend to talk, use lots of facial expressions, and keep the face active. It is not necessary to record any sound or talking for this robot face.

2. Meanwhile, place the TV and VCR on a strong, safe table.

3. An adult can cut the cardboard as directed by the artist to frame the TV screen and build the robot's body shape. The TV screen will be the robot's head.

4. Decorate the cardboard with junk, collage items, beads, and paint and things to make the robot more life-like. Parts of broken toys and machines are very robot-like and fun to use.

5. Now, with adult help, insert the tape of the animated face in the VCR. Turn it on. Push play. Look at the life-like robot with the amazing action face.

Nici Smith, age 10,
Robot Collage

Lichtenstein 1923-

Roy Lichtenstein

During the 1960's a new movement in art called Pop Op became very popular in America, owing its beginnings to Dada and Marcel Duchamp (see p.73). Like Dada, Pop is connected to using amazing wit and imagination. Roy Lichtenstein, an American art teacher and commercial artist, based his art work completely on comic strips, advertising, and bubble-gum wrappers. He did not make fun of these images. He worked very hard to reproduce comic art on a large billboard sized canvas, a very difficult job. Although he seems to be copying comics, he actually is creating them with a connection of dots and color. He often includes a white talk-balloon so the cartoon characters can say things to the viewers. Instead of working small like the size of a normal cartoon or comic, all of Lichtenstein's work is done at the scale of a great large mural painting.

To explore the approach of Pop Op artist Lichtenstein, the young artist makes dots of color on a very large sheet of paper, imitating the comic strip style of art. This challenging activity may need several tries before the artist is satisfied with the results of the experience.

*American art teacher and commercial artist Roy Lichtenstein (**LIK**-TEN-STYN) based his art works on comic strips, advertising, and bubble-gum wrappers. He liked to use words in a talk balloon like, Wham! Boom! Zap!*

Comic Dots

MATERIALS
- comic books or newspaper cartoons from a Sunday morning paper
- magnifying glass
- large sheet of butcher paper, about 4'x8', taped to the wall
- pencil
- tempera paints in red, yellow, black, or other (spread in flat grocery trays)
- round sponges, about 1/2" across
- marking pen or paintbrush

PROCESS
1. Look at a cartoon or comic with a magnifying glass. Notice all the tiny dots. See how the dots are different colors. Then take away the magnifying glass and look at the comic again. See how the colors and dots blend together to create the comic.
2. Sketch a simple comic idea – one frame or box is enough – on the butcher paper. Try for a simple character or object. Draw and outline the basic features of the character and other objects in the cartoon. Draw a talk-balloon, if desired, to hold some simple words for the comic. Or, use a large word as an exclamation, such as -
   Wow!   Pow!   Sigh!   Oh, No!
3. Now apply dots of paint about 1" apart to create a large scale picture. Fill in the character's features, such as hair and clothes, with dots of whatever color seems best. Use dots instead of lines for everything.
4. Stand back. See if the dots and colors blend. Then add more dots to complete.
5. Write the words in the balloon with a black marking pen or paint.
6. While the painting dries, stand back and look over the effect of the dots.
7. If desired, try this dot painting idea again on another sheet of paper and see how it goes the second time. This can be a fairly difficult activity, but fun to try and see how Lichtenstein was able to accomplish this challenging comic approach in grand scale art.

Warhol 1930-1987

Warhol (**WOR**-HOHL) *loved making art using the images of famous people like Elvis Presley or famous things like Campbell's soup.*

Lots of Me!

MATERIALS
- photograph of the artist
- photocopy machine
- scissors
- pencil and ruler
- colored pencils, crayons, marker pens
- 12"x18" sheet of heavy paper
- glue

PROCESS
1. Use the photocopy machine to enlarge a photo of the artist so the face of the artist can be trimmed to make a 6" square. Make 6 total copies.
   Note: Adjust the copier so the photocopies are not too dark. Adult help may be needed.
2. With adult help, measure the photocopies to 6" square and trim them so they're all the same size.
3. Lay out the identical six faces on the heavy paper.
4. With colored pencils, crayons or markers, color each of the six faces differently. Move the copies into different positions while working. Cut some of the copies differently, such as cutting all the background out of one copy, or cutting the face out of another and leaving only the background.
5. When happy with the design, glue the 6 copies in place with edges touching like a checkerboard to make a Warhol-like photo collage!

VARIATIONS
- Take pictures with a camera of close-ups of people. Work with the photographs to make a photo-collage.
- Use the enlargement feature on the copy machine to make the photo of the artist's face 200% bigger. Color or cut each face differently. Paste down the enlarged copies on a large poster-sized paper.

Andy Warhol

The American artist Andy Warhol was famous for paintings of celebrities. Warhol's paintings often start with photographs of a famous person. Many of his paintings show repeats of the same image colored in different ways. Warhol loved making art using the images of famous people and celebrities. His most famous works are pictures of movie star, Marilyn Monroe. He also created art with images of Elizabeth Taylor, Elvis Presley, and the famous red and white Campbell's soup can, an image that almost everyone knows.

The young artist creates a repeating image collage from his own photograph with the use of a photocopy machine, imitating the style of Andy Warhol.

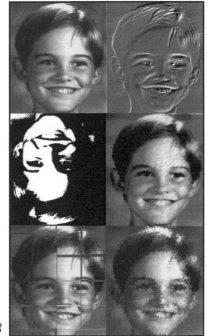

Matt Means, age 8

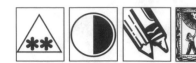

Ringgold 1930-

Faith Ringgold

Faith Ringgold grew up in the Harlem district of New York City in the 1930's. She was always known as the best artist in her class and loved to draw and paint. Her mother taught her how to sew, and Faith often tried to create her own designs with needle and thread.

Ringgold worked as a schoolteacher for many years while still creating art and trying to get her paintings accepted professionally at galleries and museums. She was inspired by pride in her African-American heritage and by many other writers and artists of the time. In the early 1970's, Ringgold began using fabric, beads, and stitched cloth in her paintings. She combined the spirit of African art with images from her childhood and black American history. Her quilted paintings are now part of many museum collections around the world.

The young artist explores creating quilted artwork by first imagining a picture that tells a story about the artist's life, and then incorporating that picture into a fabric painting in the style of Faith Ringgold.

Jodi Drost, age 9, Camping Quilt Scene

Faith Ringgold (**RING**-GOLD) creates quilts that reflect pride in her African-American heritage.

Quilted Work

MATERIALS
- piece of plain white or tan cotton cloth, about 12" x 18"
- crayons (fabric crayons or regular crayons)
- adult helper with a clothing iron
- scrap paper and a piece of aluminum foil
- many different pieces of scrap fabric
- good scissors that will easily cut cloth
- sewing machine with colorful thread, optional
- white glue
- piece of cardboard
- regular scissors
- masking tape

PROCESS
1. Draw a picture in the middle of a plain piece of cloth with crayons, leaving about 4" of plain cloth on all sides. The picture can tell a story about the artist's life. For example, draw family at the beach, show the soccer team, or draw friends playing at school. Draw any picture idea on the cloth. Press hard with the crayons to get lots of color onto the cloth.
2. Next, an adult can iron the cloth. Before ironing, place scrap paper under the crayon cloth and a piece of foil on top of it so the iron will be protected from melted crayon. Then press hard with the iron for a few minutes to melt the colored wax into the fabric and make it permanent.
3. To design a fabric frame for the drawing, cut pieces of cloth to fit around the edges of the drawing. Cut long strips of cloth, squares, triangles, or shapes. Choose favorite colors and patterns. Glue the chosen cloth pieces onto the plain fabric border until the frame is finished.
4. Optional step: With adult help and the use of a sewing machine, stitch over the fabric frame and crayon picture with colorful thread. Ringgold often sews right over the top of her painting as she frames it with quilted fabric.
5. To finish, trim some cardboard a little bit smaller than the fabric picture. Center the drawing on one side, wrap the fabric edges around to the back of the cardboard, and tape edges down with masking tape to finish.

Davis 1946-

Jim Davis (DAY-VIHS) created the famous cartoon strip, Garfield the Cat, *focusing on a storyline about a young cartoonist named Jon Arbuckle and his lazy cat, Garfield..*

Comic Creatures

MATERIALS
- large sheet of white drawing paper or newsprint
- 3 sheets of white drawing paper
- colored marking pens, pencils
- tape

PROCESS
1. Practice drawing different types of animal or imaginary characters on a large sheet of white paper. They can have large eyes like Garfield or an original characteristic like funny teeth or crazy hair. Look at the sketches and drawings and choose one character that is fun to draw and has funny possibilities. This will be the star of the new cartoon comic strip. Think of a name for the new character, too.
2. Imagine something funny that could happen to this character in three steps. For example, if the character is a spider who likes to spin webs that make pictures instead of catching bugs, maybe his name could be van Gogh, like the famous artist. In the first box he could be spinning his web natural as you please, in the second box he could be drawn with a very wild design forming, and in the third box he could be drawn wrapped up and tangled in his own design. Words could be added or left out.
3. Tape 3 sheets of white paper together in a row. Each sheet will be a box. Draw the cartoon character story into the three boxes. Color them if desired. Word balloons for talking can be added, but are not required. Talking can also be written without balloons.
4. Think up a name for the comic strip and write it on the strip like a title. Put the cartoonist's name too, just like Jim Davis and other cartoonists do. Look at some newspaper comics to see how different cartoonists do this in different ways. Create a Sunday Funnies by assembling copies of comic strips by different cartoonist children on one large sheet of newsprint for all to read. Color in, if desired.
5. Make as many comic strips as desired. Save all the comics to share with family and friends. See if they laugh and understand the humor.

Jim Davis, "Garfield"
Jim Davis is an American cartoonist famous for his amusing comic strip characters Garfield, Odie, and John, characters in the strip "Garfield". Davis draws round-eyed characters with strong personalities who are always finding something to do or say that is funny or silly. Davis' characters seem to always surprise each other, which adds to the humor of the strip.

When Davis was young, working on the family farm, he developed asthma and was confined to the house at times. He discovered that drawing helped him pass the time and found that he enjoyed drawing funny animals who talked - especially cows. When his teachers recognized his new talent, they encouraged him to take art classes.

When Davis grew up, he landed a job working for cartoonist, Tom Ryan, creator of "Tumbleweeds". Here Davis learned how to produce a daily comic strip. Later on, when his own comic strip idea "Gnom Gnat" was rejected over and over, Davis focused on a storyline about a young cartoonist named Jon Arbuckle and his lazy cat, Garfield, and the rest is history, as they say.

Young artists create new cartoon characters using pen and paper, just like Jim Davis and Garfield the Cat.

Jared Lollar, age 8, Invasion from Mars

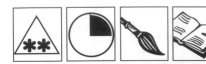

Chris Van Allsburg

Chris Van Allsburg won the Caldecott Medal in 1985 for his beautiful illustrations for the children's picture book, The Polar Express. *This is the highest honor possible for illustration of a children's book. Van Allsburg has an unusual and unique way of illustrating from different angles – from up high, from below, from the side. His work is mysterious and comforting – a feeling children seem to love. He has illustrated other imaginative books, including* Jumanji, The Wreck of the Zephyr, *and* The Garden of Abdul Gasazi.

Van Allsburg says he likes to use charcoal, pen and ink, pastel, oil pastel, and watercolor – whatever's handy and looks right to him. Sometimes he builds models of things that he is going to draw to see how shadows and light will fall on the model from different angles.

Young artists explore painting a house at night using a flashlight shining on a model house, creating lights glowing through the snow.

"I realized that as an adult I could have the same fun I had as a kid making art." – Chris Van Allsburg (VAN ALZ-BERG), from Talking with Artists, *by Pat Cummings*

Glowing House

MATERIALS
- pencil
- paints and brushes (watercolor paints work well) or other coloring tools (crayons, pastels, oil pastels)
- white or light yellow tempera paint and a brush
- large sheet of light brown, gray, or ivory drawing paper
- toy house for a model (or a milk carton or wood block)
- flashlight to create shadows

PROCESS
1. Look at the book, *The Polar Express*, to see how Van Allsburg uses color for windows, moonlight, and snow at night. He uses yellow for windows in buildings and the train, snow and stars are dots of yellow, white, or blue. Look at the dark and light in his drawings.
2. Next, set up a model of a house on the table. Use a milk carton, a block, or a toy house. Turn down the lights. Shine a flashlight on the house model, noting where the light is brightest and where the shadows fall. Then prop up the light so hands will be free for drawing.
3. Begin a sketch of the house on the drawing paper. Lightly use the pencil to shade in some of the shadows.
4. Next, paint or color in the house. Use white or yellow to indicate bright light. Use darker colors to indicate shadows.
5. Paint or color in other areas of the drawing.
6. Now, with white or yellow tempera paint, add lights in the windows, add stars, or add snow. Paint it on in dots or small spots for snow or far away stars. Paint in solid shapes for brightly lit windows. Let dry. Does the house seem to glow in the night?

MAKE IT & PLAY IT

chapter 5

Games
& Activities

Great Artists Cards

Famous artists and great masters are included in a home-made card game that will help young artists learn and remember things about their favorite famous artists.

MATERIALS
- small prints of famous paintings (from postcards, note cards, magazines, catalogs, and museum brochures)
- 3"x5" index cards
- glue stick
- scissors
- pen
- Con-Tact Clear Cover™ or clear wide shipping tape, optional

PROCESS
1. Cut out and collect small pictures of famous paintings.
2. Glue each of these pictures onto an index card.
3. On the back of each card, write any or all of the following:
   > the name of the artist
   > the name of the artwork
   > the date it was painted
   > the type of art it is (landscape, portrait, abstract, etc.).
4. The cards will last longer if each glued-on picture card is covered with a layer of Con-Tact Clear Cover™ or clear wide shipping tape.
5. When enough art cards are completed, there are several card games which can be played. Play games similar to *Go Fish* or *Rummy* by dealing the cards out to several players, then laying down cards in sets of three (3 Renoir paintings, 3 portraits, 3 landscapes, 3 paintings from the 1890's, and so on). The rules can be set to fit the cards in the collection.

VARIATIONS
- Use the cards as tiny posters. Hang them anywhere they can be enjoyed, such as in a bedroom, on the refrigerator, or taped to the bathroom mirror.
- Use the cards as flash cards to learn the names of artists and great paintings in a rapid-fire game of *Memory* or *Concentration*.
- Use the cards as part of the Map of Honor (p.124-125) or other games in this chapter.

Masters Match

MATERIALS
- art postcards
- photocopy machine
- scissors
- glue
- any clear adhesive, such as, Con-Tact Clear Cover™ or wide shipping tape
- poster board for base of game

Young artists construct a matching game made with art postcards of famous masterpieces and the use of a photocopy machine. Being familiar with the art of the great masters becomes an enjoyable game when part of everyday playtime.

PROCESS
To construct game –
1. Collect postcards of the masterpieces from sources such as the Metropolitan Museum of Art catalog or a local bookstore or stationery store. (Sometimes they come in a tear-out book of 30 or more postcards.)
2. Place about 4 to 6 postcards (or however many will fit) on the photocopy machine. Make a black and white copy of the postcards. Then remove the cards.
3. Place more cards on the machine and photocopy these. Repeat this until there are sufficient cards for the game (a minimum of six and a maximum of 100).
4. Cut them apart on the natural lines made from the rectangular postcards.
5. Place the art photocopies on the posterboard and stick with only a drop of glue to hold. Then cover the entire board with clear adhesive Con-Tact Clear Cover™ or strips of wide, clear shipping tape to protect and preserve.

To play –
Basic play for one –
1. Hold or spread out the postcards and then match each postcard on its identical black and white photocopy on the board.
2. Play until the board is full.

Basic play for two to four –
1. Deal or pass out the postcards to all the players.
2. Players take turns placing a postcard on the photocopy on the board.
   Or, place a stack of postcards on the floor. The first player will turn over the first card and then match it to the photocopy. The next player then turns over the next card and matches it. And so on.
3. Play until all cards are matched.

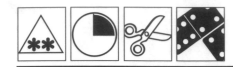

Master-Puzzlepiece

Young artists construct their own puzzles with small art prints of famous masterpieces. Becoming more familiar with the art of the great masters is easier and simpler when part of the young artist's playtime.

MATERIALS
- 1 or more small prints or pictures from magazines or catalogs of the art of the great masters (photocopies of the small prints work well, too)
- matte board
- glue
- pencil
- scissors
- manila envelope or small box

PROCESS
1. Glue the small art print to a piece of matte board.
2. Dry thoroughly.
3. Turn the matte board over.
4. The young artist and the adult can draw puzzle pieces on the back of the puzzle (no more than 10 and no less than two).
   Note: Cutting the print in half is a two-piece puzzle that is more of a matching activity ideal for very young children. More than two pieces is appropriate for children who are more experienced with puzzles.
5. An adult can carefully cut the puzzle into pieces.
6. Assemble the puzzle over and over.
7. Keep the puzzle in the manila envelope or small box.

VARIATION
- Mix two or more puzzles together on the table and then sort and assemble the puzzles back together again.

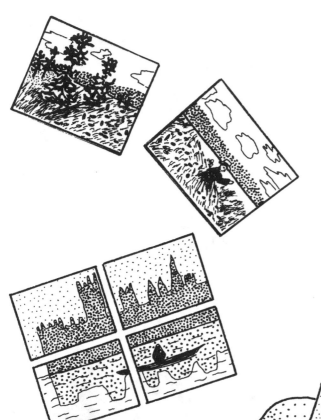

Masters Scrap Book

MATERIALS
- scrap book (commercial or homemade)
- paste, glue, or tape
- scissors
- empty box for storage of clippings
- any of the following art resources -

    museum catalogs   gift catalogs with art prints   art stationery catalogs
    art postcards   photocopies of art works   Smithsonian magazines

PROCESS
1. Collect images, clippings, and photocopies of great art works. Keep them in a big box until ready to use.
2. Sort through the art works, finding those that are going to be saved in the scrap book. Each child will have his or her own way to sort and save their favorite or most interesting works of art. Think up a way to sort them, such as by -

    artist's name or portrait
    colors (bright or soft)
    landscapes or people
    Impressionists or Cubists
    funny or sad
    delicate or abstract

    There are many, many ways to save the art clippings. Some children like to save as many as they can on each page with no particular sorting style.
3. Paste, glue, or tape the art works into the scrap book.
4. Keep adding to the scrap book over time. This project will not be finished in one day.

VARIATIONS
- Save original drawings and paintings created by the scrap book owner in the scrap book.
- Save photographs of paintings, sculpture, or other works of art seen in real life in museums or on walks through local galleries.

When children have become familiar with famous works of art, many of them will develop favorites, much like the way kids collect baseball cards or stickers! Provide museum catalogs, magazines, and school supply catalogs that sell art prints and stationery. The young artists cut out their favorite works by the great masters and paste them into a scrap book, sorting and organizing in a way meaningful to that child. Some children like to name a scrap book page after a famous artist and find artworks by that artist to glue on that page. Other children have a more random style of organization. Some young artists like to paste-in their own personal art works to go along with the others they are saving! Adults can help by photocopying art works from art books and giving them to the collector to add to the scrap book.

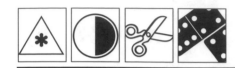

Smart Art Cards

Some children are ready to pair a postcard of each great artist's most famous works with the artist's name and face. This easy-to-make game helps young artists do just that, and become "art smart".

MATERIALS
- art postcards
- posterboard, tag board, or heavy paper
- look-alike sketches or photographs or photocopies of selected famous artists
- Con-Tact Clear Cover™, optional
- photocopy machine
- colored pencils, optional
- scissors
- glue or paste
- permanent marking pen
- rubber band, box, or envelope

PROCESS
To make the "Smart Art" game –
1. Look through this book or other sources for photographs, paintings, or sketches of famous artists that show what they looked like, especially their faces. Photocopy a selection of favorite famous artists.
   Note: Enlarge the photocopy of the artist's face and then color it in with colored pencils, if desired.
2. Next, cut out the faces and paste or glue each one to a square of posterboard or heavy paper that will fit the artist's face size. Usually a piece 6"x9" works well, but any size is fine. With a permanent black pen, label the artist's name in clear, bold letters on the card.
3. To protect the card, cover the face and name with a piece Con-Tact Clear Cover™ cut a little larger than the face and name card. Fold over and stick the extra Con-Tact™ around to the back of the card for a good protective cover. These cards are called the "Artist Cards".
4. Select postcards of famous artworks (or photocopy famous works from books) done by the artist selected for the Artist Cards. To make the game more challenging, find more than one art work for each artist. These are called the "Artworks Cards".
5. To store the Smart Art game, find a box, large envelope, or a heavy rubber band to hold the cards and postcards together.

Smart Art Cards continued

To play "Smart Art Sort", for one person, or any number of friends –

1. Spread out the Artist Cards on a clear work space on the floor or on a table.
2. Go through the Artworks Cards or postcards of famous artworks and try to match the artwork to the artist who created the work. (See illustration for a suggested way to sort the cards out on the table.)

To play "Smart Art Match", for two –

1. Deal out the Artist Cards between two players. Each player spreads his Artist Cards out in front of him.
2. Place the stack of Artworks Cards (postcards) in the middle of the two players, picture side down.
3. The first player draws a postcard from the deck. If it matches one of the Artist Cards, place the postcard on top of the Artist Card it matches. If it does not match an artist, place it picture side up next to the stack of post cards. The other player may match this postcard to an artist he has at this time.
4. The other player draws a postcard from the deck. If it matches, keep it. If it does not match, turn it picture side up next to the deck. The other player then can take it and match, or leave it where it is.
5. Play until all the postcards have been used. No one necessarily needs to win. If winning is important, count up the number of postcard matches for a score. The one with the most artworks matching artists wins.

Great Art Cookies

Basic sugar cookies are painted with an egg-yolk and food coloring paint mixture in the style of a famous artist. For example, artists can create Pollock Spatter Cookies, Mondrian Geometric Cookies, Picasso Cubist Cookies, Van Gogh Starry Night Cookies, and O'Keeffe Flower Cookies. Bake and enjoy as part of a Great Artist Cookies and Milk Party. This recipe makes about 4 dozen normal sized cookies, or 12 extra large art cookies.

MATERIALS
Basic Sugar Cookie Recipe –
- 3/4 cup butter or margarine, softened (1/4 lb. plus 4 T.)
- 1 cup sugar
- 2 eggs
- 1 t. vanilla
- 2-3/4 cups all-purpose flour
- 1 t. baking powder and 1 t. salt
- sugar for sprinkling
- measuring cups
- electric mixer
- 2 bowls
- measuring spoons
- floured board
- rolling pin
- refrigerator
- plastic wrap
- cookie cutter or dull knife
- hot pads
- cooling racks
- baking sheet
- spatula
- oven preheated to 375°F

Other cookie supplies –
- 1 egg-yolk per cup
- small cup per color
- food coloring, one color per cup
- small, clean paint brushes
- fork to mix
- covered work area
- napkins for each person
- glass of milk for each person
- optional decorations: raisins, chocolate chips, coconut, seeds

Note: Ready-made frozen sugar cookie dough is available at the grocery store and can be used in place of home made dough.

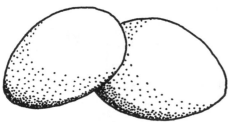

Great Art Cookies continued

Prepare the Basic Sugar Cookie recipe –

Beat until creamy 3/4 cup butter and 1 cup sugar in the large bowl with the electric mixer. Beat in the 2 eggs and 1 t. vanilla. In the other bowl, stir together 2-3/4 cup flour, 1 t. baking powder, and 1 t. salt. Gradually add the flour mixture to the sugar-butter, blending and forming a soft dough. Cover the dough with plastic wrap and refrigerate for at least 1 hour and for up to 3 days. Divide the dough into 12 equal portions. Roll out each portion on the floured board until about 1/8" thick. Each artist can cut a cookie cutter circle from this portion, or use a dull knife to cut out any shape. Lift the excess dough and save for making additional cookies.

Prepare the paint, one egg for each color needed –

Separate each egg and let the yolk fall into a small, clean cup. Save the white for cooking, or discard. Stir the egg yolk with a little bit of water using the fork. Then add drops of food coloring into the yolk to reach a desired color, stirring the color in with the fork. Prepare one cup with one egg yolk for each color needed.

PROCESS

1. Sprinkle the work surface with a little bit of flour. Place the sugar cookie shape on the lightly floured work surface. Think of the styles of different great artists and choose a style to paint on the cookie.
2. Paint and decorate the cookies in the style of a great artist. Further decorate with toppings such as raisins, chocolate chips, nuts, coconut, or seeds. For example, Pollock is known for splattering color, Picasso is known for painting cubist designs, Stella might decorate with a line design, and O'Keeffe would probably paint a large, bright flower. Artists with a recognizable style are the most fun to imitate when designing art cookies.
3. Gently move the painted cookie to the baking sheet. Sprinkle generously with sugar.
4. When the baking sheet is full, and with adult help, bake the cookies for 8-10 minutes at 375°F or until the edges are lightly browned.
5. Using a spatula, remove the cookies from the baking sheet to individual napkins.
6. To eat and enjoy, throw a Great Art Cookies and Milk Party for all the great cookie artists (while cookies are still warm – mmmm). Cookies can be stored airtight for several days.

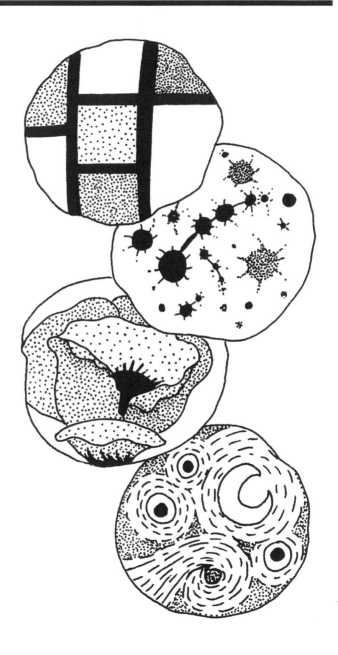

Great Art Dominoes

Kids clip small photos of paintings and sculptures out of magazines and glue them on small blocks of wood or cardboard rectangles. Play a traditional domino game of matching end to end images.

MATERIALS
- rectangles shapes made from any of the following –
  - heavy cardboard
  - wood scraps
  - wood blocks

Note: Most small children like rectangles cut large (about 3"x6" or larger) most older kids like them cut small (about 1"x2" or domino size)

- small images of paintings and sculptures clipped from any of the following (clip 2 of each image) –
  - museum gift catalogs
  - art poster catalog
  - old Smithsonian magazines
  - teacher supply catalogs
  - catalogs selling small art prints, art note cards and stationery, art T-shirts, etc.
- glue to attach the clippings to the rectangles (an alternative to glue is wide shipping tape or Clear Con-Tact ™ to cover the clippings and seal them on the rectangles)
- scissors

PROCESS
To make the dominoes –

1. Look through old gift catalogs, art poster catalogs, or other magazines for images of famous works of art. Clip as many as possible, looking for two of each that will match.

2. Trim images to fit half of the cardboard or wood scrap rectangles on hand.

3. Spread glue on the back of one clipping and press it to half of the rectangle. Spread glue on the matching clipping and press it to half of another rectangle. Spread glue on the rest of the clippings, filling in the rectangle halves.
   Note: Instead of glue, wide shipping tape or Clear Con-Tact ™ can be used to attach the clippings to the rectangles, wrapping the tape over the clippings and around the back of the rectangle, sealing in the clipping.

4. If there is an art image with at least four identical clippings, make a domino that is "doubles"; that is, a domino with both images on either end the same. The other two matching clippings can be used on two other dominoes. (Single images can also make a domino pair – half of the painting on one domino, half on another domino. Matching these dominoes completes the image like a 2-piece puzzle.)

Great Art Dominoes continued

To play and explore with the dominoes, but not a game –

1. Build, match, sort, enjoy freely with no rules.

To play a game of art dominoes, for one –

1. Spread out all the dominoes on the floor or table.
2. Begin with one domino (officially a "double" domino should be used to start) and then choose another one that matches. Bring the two matching identical art images together end to end.
3. Next, match another domino to either of the images that do not have a matching domino yet. Continue matching images and adding dominoes to the design made by the rectangles.
4. The game is over when the single player has matched all the dominoes or when the design made by the dominoes is satisfactory to the player.

To play a game of art dominoes, for two or more –

1. Deal out dominoes equally to each person until all the dominoes are used.
2. The player who has a double places that domino on the floor or table.
3. The next person matches a domino to that one. If he doesn't have a matching one, he must wait until his next turn. The next player matches, if possible, and so on.
4. Play until dominoes are used up. Or, play to win: the winner is the first one with no dominoes left.

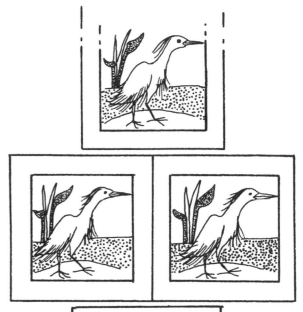

Great Art Coloring Pages

A group of kids make their own coloring books by each one tracing the main shapes of a favorite art print. The tracings are then photocopied for as many children as will have a coloring book, and all the copies are put into individual coloring books.

MATERIALS
- sheets of clear acrylic plastic (or a piece of tracing paper)
- tape
- permanent black markers
- art prints
- photo copy machine with white paper (regular 8"x10")
- stapler
- large sheets of construction paper (16"x20")
- crayons

PROCESS
Note: For this group project, each child chooses a favorite famous art print and traces it. All the tracings when photocopied will make up the coloring book for each child.

1. Place a sheet of clear acrylic or tracing paper over a chosen art print. Tape the corners of the acrylic sheet to the table (but not to the print) to help keep the wiggles out of the tracing.
2. Trace the main shapes of the art print with a bold permanent black marking pen.
3. An adult photocopies the traced image, making as many copies as there are children in the group.
4. When all the children in the group have had their tracings photocopied, one copy of each tracing is placed in a stack for each child.
5. To make a cover for the coloring book, fold a large sheet of construction paper down the middle. Each child can decorate the cover with the marking pen and crayons and the name of the child.
6. Place the stack of coloring pages inside the cover. Staple down the folded edge of the cover, making sure the coloring pages are also being stapled inside.
7. Fold open the coloring book, choose a page, and begin coloring.

Simplified Versions
- An adult can photocopy children's favorite art prints or copies from books or catalogs, making one copy for each child. Most photocopy machines have the capability to reduce or enlarge the size of the art to fit on a regular 8"x10" sheet of paper. Staple the copies of the art into a book for each child which they can color-in with crayons, pencils, or marking pens.
- Each child draws with a black pen on white paper to make a coloring book. The adult then makes photocopies of these black and white drawings for the entire group and staples them into coloring book pages for each child:
    - any drawing at all
    - a drawing of a favorite art print from memory

Great Time Line

Young artists easily understand the development of art through the ages when they make an Art Time Line "clothesline" or wall display. Set up the time line in a permanent location and add to it as new artists and eras are explored.

MATERIALS
- a piece of twine or stout string 6' to 10' long
- nails or hooks to hang the string as a "clothesline"
- key tags from an office supply store punched with a hole
- tape, paper clips, black marking pen
- small pictures of famous artworks clipped from resources, such as -
  art magazines   museum catalogs   art postcards

PROCESS
1. Fold the string in half 3 or 4 times and make a mark at the folds. When unfolded there will be equally spaced sections (7 marks if 3 folds were made, or 15 marks if 4 folds were made). Equal spaces can be marked with a ruler, if desired.
2. Make date tags for the art era of choice. Make a marker for each 500 years, starting with the present day (2000AD) and going backwards (1500AD, 1000AD, 500AD, year 500BC and so on back to the Egyptian era of 3000BC). Tie a date tag onto the string at each equally spaced mark. If studying a more recent period of history, adjust the date markers accordingly (for instance, a marker for each 100 years between 1000AD and today's 2000AD, or a marker for every decade from 1900 to today). Create a time line to fit the artist's choices.
4. As new artists and works of art are explored, cut a small example from a magazine or museum catalog and write the date of the artwork on the back. Then, using a paperclip, "hang" the picture on the clothesline at the appropriate location.

VARIATION
- A wall display time line can be made using a length of adding machine paper divided into equal sections, labeled with appropriate years, and taped along a wall, perhaps down a long hallway. Clippings can be attached with tags or tape.
  Note: Most known artworks will be found at the very end of the time line in the recent decades, but children like to "see" the length of time that has passed when they place more ancient works along the line. Although impractical to stretch a clothesline far enough to include prehistoric arts from 15,000BC, it's fun for kids to figure out how far out the back door a time line would have to stretch to do just that.

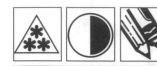

Happy Birthday, Mr. Picasso

Children love to celebrate birthdays. The dates of birth of many great artists are the perfect opportunity to celebrate and enjoy the art of special artists throughout the year. Young artists can record birthdays on any calendar at home or at school with stickers and child-decorated labels. The rest of the celebration ideas are the choice of the young artist!

MATERIALS
- calendar with big, open squares
- tape or glue, optional
- sticky dots
- stick-on blank shipping labels, about 3"x5" (use squares of paper or index cards)
- marking pens
- other pens or pencils
- scissors

PROCESS
To put together the calendar:
1. Look in the Resource Guide, p.138, and find the birthday list. Choose some favorite artists and their birthdays, or choose them all!
2. Spread open a calendar with open squares for the days with a blank or unimportant matching page for the art.
3. Draw on a large blank label to show the style of that artist. For example, for Van Gogh draw some swirling stars or a sunflower in a vase. For Pollock, draw some splashes and droplets of paint. For Picasso, draw some cubes or a funny sideways face. It can be difficult to draw in such a small space, but enjoy trying to capture the style of that artist in any way. Or, simply write the name of the artist on the label and decorate around the name. Another idea would be to cut out a print from a catalog or magazine of something done by that artist and glue that on the label instead of drawing.
4. Go to the calendar and turn the pages to the correct month and birthday of the chosen artist. Stick the label on the calendar as shown in the illustration, not on the numbers, but on the matching page. It may be necessary to cover other art or images on the calendar. Be sure this is okay with the calendar owner.
5. Then, place a colorful sticky-dot on the corresponding date square of the calendar that matches the birthday of the artist. Write the artist's name too, if desired. The calendar will be a daily and monthly reminder of famous artists and their wonderful works.

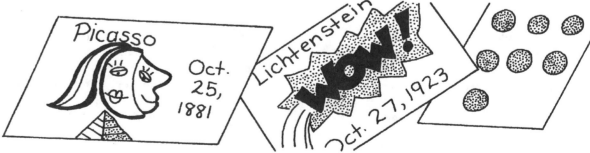

Happy Birthday continued

To celebrate the birthdays:

When the birthday of each artist comes around, there could be many ways to celebrate the special day.

Here are several ideas:

1. Do an art project in the style of that artist on his birthday.
2. Look back at old art projects and find one done in the style of that artist to put up on the wall in a place of honor.
3. Look at a book and spend time finding artworks by that artist.
4. Put up an art poster on the wall for the day or the rest of the month. Libraries have art prints on loan for just such occasions.
5. Go for a walk and look for scenes that look like something that artist might have painted.
6. Send a pretend birthday card to the artist. If the artist is still living, consider sending a real birthday card to the real person!
7. Sing happy birthday to the artist.
8. Have some cake and icecream or other treats to celebrate the day.
9. Make Great Art Cookies (p.114-115) in the style of the birthday artist.

Gallery Walk

Young artists construct permanent frames to display their personal paper artworks, such as their own paintings and drawings, or art prints of famous artists' works. The artworks can be changed daily or at any time for an interchangeable gallery showing. Display is part of the enjoyment of art for young and old alike. Constructing the frames is part of the creative art work.

Rob Harweger, age 8,
Gallery Picture

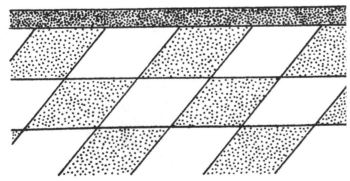

MATERIALS
- favorite child-made art work or print of famous artwork
- any choice of cardboard or heavy paper, such as -

matte board	posterboard	tagboard
formboard	cardboard	wooden frame

- scissors
- yardstick, ruler, or straight edge
- marking pens
- optional decorative collage materials to apply with white glue, such as -

beads	wrapping paper	buttons
art tissue scraps	toothpicks	paint & brushes
confetti, sequins, other little things		glitter

- metallic paint, such as gold, and a brush
- Con-Tac Clear Cover™, optional
- squeezy poster display clay

PROCESS
1. Place a piece of heavy cardboard or matte board on the floor. With adult help, draw a square or rectangle in the center of the board. Cut out this square so a hole is left. Set aside the square for further use.
2. To decorate the remaining frame, decide on any method of choice, such as -
   - colored and decorate as is
   - glue fancy wrapping paper over the frame shape
   - decorate with beads and glitter like jewels
   - decorate with other collage items
   - paint glittering and gold
   - paint with designs
3. Let the decoration dry, if needed.
4. Choose an artwork that fits the frame. Squeeze some tacky poster display clay into eight little balls. Stick the art work to the wall with four balls, one for each corner of the artwork.
5. Then stick the frame to the wall around the artwork with the remaining four balls of poster display clay. More may be needed if the frame is very heavy.
6. Display the framed artworks on a prominent, important wall for all to see. For a gallery look, display many framed works of art all in a row. When ready, remove each art work and place a new one in the frame for a changing gallery showing.

Masterpiece Montage

MATERIALS
- found, collected, and selected dramatic props and costumes, such as –

hats	coats	dresses	glasses	boas
shoes	boots	jewelry	hairdos	chairs

- stuffed toys and dolls, such as –

horses	dogs	cows	lions	babies

- a "stage" area to dramatize the masterpiece montage
- a backdrop, optional (such as an old sheet, a big open piece of cardboard, a blank wall)

PROCESS
1. Look through masterpieces by the great masters and other artists. Choose one that would be fun to "act out" in a frozen, still montage. For example, one of Renoir's paintings called *The Swing* would need four people to create the montage: One girl in a fancy dress to pretend she is on a swing, two boys in farmer clothing to pose nearby and watch, and a young child to stand to the side wishing she could swing too. Another example would be a painting by Édouard Manet called *The Balcony*. This montage would need: one man in a suit and tie to stand on the balcony, and two women in fancy white dresses to sit in the foreground, one with a fan and one with an umbrella. A stuffed toy of a dog placed at the feet of the woman with the fan would add to the montage.
2. Dress up in the props or costumes that go with that painting.
3. Stand or arrange each other like the characters in the painting. Hold very still. Don't even laugh or smile unless the character is supposed to.
4. Others may guess what artist's work is being acted out in this montage, and may even be able to name the painting itself.

VARIATIONS
- Take a picture of each montage to compare to the great works of art later.
- Use puppets to act out a made up story that will go with a painting.
- Make up a story to go with a painting and act out an entire made up story.

Young artists collect costumes and props that go with a favorite masterpiece. Then they dress up like the characters in the painting or sculpture and pose still as rocks, as if they were in a painting. Holding very still is part of the challenge. For additional fun, others can guess which artist's work is being dramatized in the still montage, and possibly even the name the artist gave the work of art.

Map of Honor

Great artists have lived all over the world in many different countries and continents, from the dawn of man until the present day. Find out where favorite artists lived or worked and plot it on a map of the world. When a particular artist or art style is explored, that artist can be placed on the map of honor.

MATERIALS
- large sheet of cardboard, rectangular
- colored paper, optional
- string or thread
- map pins or other pins
- postcards of artist's great works
- marking pens
- scissors, tape, glue
- book with map of the world
- piece of craft paper to cover cardboard
- pencil with eraser
- foamboard, optional
- yardstick

Note: This project uses cardboard and craft paper, commonly available art materials. As a more expensive option, purchase white foamboard from an art or hobby store because it is so easy to work with. Either approach makes a great panel map.

PROCESS
1. Place the large sheet of cardboard on the floor. To make a free standing panel map, with adult help, measure and divide the rectangle into thirds, with the middle third the largest of the three. There will be two side panels and a larger middle panel. (See illustration.)
2. To score the cardboard so the panels will bend, with adult help, place the yardstick on a dividing line and gently score the cardboard with a scissors point along that line from top to bottom. Repeat this step on the other dividing line.
3. Gently fold the side panels in on the scored lines. Now the panel can stand on its own.

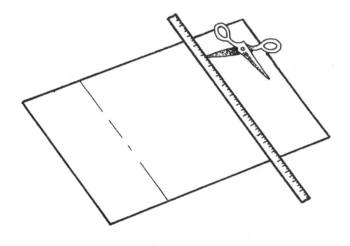

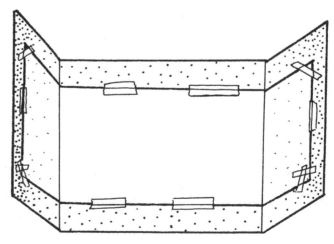

Map of Honor continued

To prepare the map:

1. Cover the cardboard with craft paper, using tape or glue to hold. Add some glue along the panel lines and edges of the cardboard so the paper won't be loose. The craft paper can fold around the edges of the cardboard (like wrapping a present) and can be glued or taped on the back of the cardboard. Option: Buy a world map at the store and tape it to the cardboard instead of drawing a map.
2. Find a map of the world in a book. Place the cardboard flat on the floor and sketch the continents of the world on the craft paper. Sketch lightly. Erasing may be necessary. This is a difficult step and may take a few days.
3. When the world is in place, continents and countries can be drawn and colored-in with marking pens. Or, for added color and arms that aren't quite so tired, cut out the shapes of countries and continents from colored scrap paper and glue in place on the map. Add in major cities, if desired. Dry.
4. Stand the map up on the floor or on a table with panels folded slightly in.

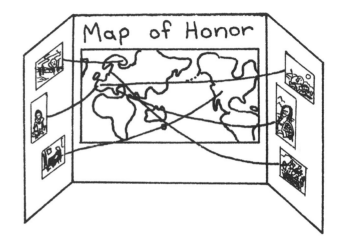

To plot the works of the artists:

1. Choose an artist of interest or one whose style has been explored through hands-on art.
2. Look in *Great Artists* or another source about artists and read to find out in which country the artist lived or worked. Then find that country on the map. Stick a pin in that country. If the city is also known, the pin can go into the city.
3. Tie a string to the pin and gently let the string out to the edge of the map. Snip the string.
4. Glue a postcard or cut-out of a work of art by that artist to the edge of the map. Tape or glue the end of the string to the picture. Additional information can be written on a scrap of paper and glued next to the art work.

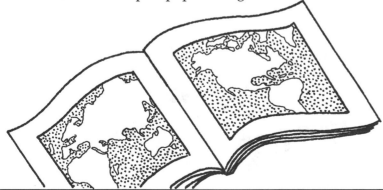

You and Me Notebook

Create a notebook to save special works of art that will compare and highlight one great artist to another. The child's artwork goes on one side, and the famous artist's in the same style goes on the other, each protected within plastic sleeves from an office supply store.

MATERIALS
- 3 ring binder
- plastic sleeves or sheet protectors (clear plastic envelope pages) for 3 ring binders
- artworks by child (or photographs of child's artworks)
- collection of clippings, postcards, or copies of famous art
- scissors, glue, and tape optional

PROCESS
1. Fill a three ring binder with any number of plastic sleeves.
2. To save a child's piece of art, slip it into a plastic sleeve.
3. On the facing page, slip in a clipping or postcard of the famous artist's work that corresponds in style. For example, if the child paints a starry night picture in the swirling style of van Gogh, the facing page in the notebook would show a clipping of the actual *The Starry Night* painting. Or, if the young artist has painted in the geometric style of Mondrian, the child's art will be saved on one page, and a copy or clipping of Mondrian's will be saved on the other.
4. Label both pages of artworks, if desired. Note: This project works especially well for saving photographs of very large sculptures or artworks that are otherwise difficult to save due their sizes.

VARIATIONS
- The notebook could be used for *photographs only* — a photo-album of the child's experiences with each great artist in art.
- Use the plastic sleeves and three ring binder for other ways to display a child's artworks.

Melinda de Bruin, age 8,
Notebook Picture

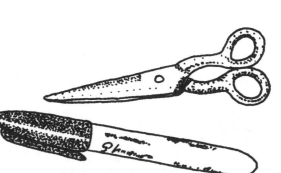

RESOURCE GUIDE
chapter 6

Great Art Words

Throughout the activities in this book, many new words and ideas are explored. Brief explanations and descriptions are listed here to help answer questions and clearly describe terms.

-A-

abstract art – art that is geometric in design or simplified from it's natural appearance; abstract art does not need to look like anything real

 Abstract–Expressionism – 1930-45 & 1946-60
two phases: Early c.1930-45 and Classic c. 1946-60; stresses spontaneity and individuality; famous examples are Kandinsky and Pollock; paint techniques might include throwing paint; interpretations are highly imaginary

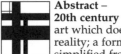 **Abstract – 20th century**
art which does not represent reality; a form that has been simplified from its original, or that is geometric in presentation and design; Mondrian is an example of an abstract artist

action painting – a painting method (employed by the artist Pollock) that uses movement to fling or throw paint onto the canvas

ancient – very old, antiquated, and from early history

apprentice – in years past, a student in art who lives, works, and studies with a master to become an artist by trade and career; was given room, board and a small allowance while learning

archeologist – someone who studies the past and learns from the fossils, pots, art, and other artifacts ancient people have left behind

architect – a person who designs and creates buildings, houses, and structures

art elements – the visual components that artists use to create, such as, shape, texture, space, line, and color

art medium – materials used in creating an art work; examples are paint, crayon, paper, clay, wire, and so on

assemblage – an art process where three-dimensional materials are joined together to build up an art work

authentic – a real, genuine, and legally official art work

-B-

background – the part of a painting or picture that appears farthest away from the viewer of the art

Baroque – a term used to describe extremely ornate decor, such as the furniture of the Palace of Versailles under King Louis the 14th

 Baroque Period – 1600-1750
an era of art and architecture known by its heavily ornate decor found in reliefs, sculptures, and other art details often bursting forth in the interiors of buildings and on furniture and walls; the Palace of Versailles is one of the best examples of Baroque decor; great Baroque painters were the Dutch Masters Rembrandt and Rubens who used heavy detail and dramatic lighting, facial expression, and depth of feeling

blob – a mass of shape or color, created with art materials such as ink or paint on paper; no particular shape but can appear to take on the appearance of real things

-C-

canvas – fabric stretched over a wood frame to paint on; often refers to any surface on which paintings are created

casting – impressions; a method of making three-dimensional sculptures by pouring a hardening liquid or melted material into a mold with that impression

center of interest – in a painting, objects, colors, and designs can be placed in a way to draw the eye to one area of interest in the work

ceramic – pottery art; works of clay glazed and then baked in a kiln

chisel – a tool in art for carving stone or clay; usually has a sharp edge at one end and is hit with a hammer on the other end

clay – an art material found in the earth which can be purchased (sometimes called Moist Clay); may also refer to other modeling compounds such as Plasticine™, Sculpey™, or DAS™, which are used like clay but are not an earth clay

cloudscape – a painting or picture where the clouds in the sky fill the paper and are the main subject of the art work

collage – art work made by cutting up various materials - string, fabric, newspaper, photos, cardboard, bits of paintings and drawings - and putting them together with glue or other bonding material; a technique used by Cubists, Dadaists, and Surrealists; Matisse is famous for this technique

collection – objects and materials are saved and grouped together to be used in collages, assemblages, or combines.

chalk – an art material made of talc and pigment pressed into sticks for coloring; some chalk is used on sidewalks or chalk boards; chalks for fine art are called pastels

combine – a type of art similar to collage and assemblage where a collection of objects or materials are combined to create a work of art; Rauschenberg is famous for combines

 comic strip – a humorous art form printed with tiny dots of color; when the dots are viewed at a normal range, the dots appear to blend and create a unified colorful picture or a series of pictures that tell a story; Jim Davis is famous for creating the "Garfield" comic strip

commercial artist – an artist who creates advertisements, posters, commercials, or other materials for promoting and selling products

 Contemporary or Modern – the present time
a term used to describe an artist who is living and creating in the present time; Nam June Paik and Christo are contemporary artists at the writing of this book (1997)

contraption – a sculpture or art work that is similar to inventions and may or may not have any use, usually overdone in scope and presentation; can be humorous or filled with fascinating, imaginary details

 Cubism, Cubist – 1907-1914
the first abstract art style of the 20th Century; instead of art that was realistic or representational, art was expressed with neutral color and geometric form; Cubists tried to create a new way of seeing things from every angle at once; the most famous Cubists are Picasso and Braque

cylinder – a three-dimensional form that is like a rounded tube or pipe in any variety of dimensions, heights, and widths

Great Art Words continued

Dada, Dadaist –
off and on through 1916-1960
an artistic movement started in 1916 by painters and poets; Dada is a non-sense word like "googoo", meaning "hobby horse" in French, meant to convey how unimportant the expression of life could be depicted in art; Dadaists were known as brilliant innovators and free-thinkers; the most famous, Marcel Duchamp, was an inventive, playful artist who believed in "happy accidents", like his art technique of dropping pieces of string on a sheet of paper and then capturing their designs in any variety of art techniques; Meret Oppenheim is most famous for her fur-lined tea cup and saucer

De Stijl –
1917-1931
a group of artists who liked to use basic forms like cubes, verticals, and horizontals in art; most De Stijl artists are considered Abstract; art is linear and plain with primary colors only, no depth or shading, sometimes nothing more than a flat grid; Piet Mondrian is the most famous De Stijl artist

Dutch Master – during the Baroque period, the greatest Dutch Masters of all time were Rembrant (1606-69, the great genius of Dutch art) and Rubens (who became a master in 1598)

-E-

earthenware – pottery made out of clay dug from the earth, then fired or baked until hard; terra cotta is type of unglazed reddish earthenware used for sculpture, pottery, and as a building material

egg tempera paint – ground colors or piments mixed with egg yolk instead of oil; used often by Italian panel painting before the 16th C.; powdered tempera paints can be mixed with water and used for children's art

enlarged – when an object or drawing is made bigger, such as when a picture is placed on a photocopy machine and then printed larger than the original

environment – all of the surroundings, climate, or habitat of one particular area; in art, sometimes considered a scene that is painted with all its details

era – a period of time; an age; one of the most famous art eras was the Renaissance

expression – the interpretation of inner emotion, vision, or strong feeling

Expressionism, Expressionist –
1900's
reality is distorted with the expression of the artists' inner emotions and visions; emotional impact is created by painting with strong brushstrokes and colors, expressing emotion and feeling regarding a chosen subject; violent colors, abstract forms, emotional subjects to express the mind; Van Gogh and Gauguin were the first; other famous Expressionists were Matisse, Kandinsky, and Rousseau

-F-

Fantastic Art –
1940's
a modern style of art similar to Surrealism; a combination of Cubism mixed with rich imagination based on childhood memories, folklore, and country life; Chagall is the best known for his paintings based on Jewish folktales and theater scenes with bright color, fantasy, and abstraction

Fauvism –
early 1900's
a style of painting where colors are the central, over-riding theme of the art work with flat pattern and bold free color; Matisse is the most famous; this style gave way to Cubism a few years later

Fimo™ – a type of plastic clay, highly managable, that can be baked hard; available in many colors; works well for fine work or beads

Folk Art – works of art that are created by people that are not professionally trained in art and used in everyday life

freeform – shapes and form with no geometric control; not regular; young children often use this style in sculpture, collage, painting, drawing, and other techniques

fresco – Italian meaning "fresh"; a painting on wet plaster where the plaster of the wall absorbs the moist paint and it becomes a permanent part of the wall

-G-

genius – an exceptionally intelligent or talented person, such as Leonardo da Vinci or Michelangelo

geometric – forms that are regular and based on shapes such as a square, circle, rectangle, triangle as well as cube, sphere, pyramid, or cylinder

geometric designs – art works created with geometric shapes as the primary form of the creation

Gothic –
12th and 13th C. Middle Ages
a general term that applies to all art in the Middle Ages; refers mostly to churches and architecture characterized by the pointed arch and use of extensive glass; sculpture and stained glass were incorporated in Gothic architecture; clarity of design and structure; called the Age of the Great Cathedrals; the most famous is Notre-Dame in Paris; Late Gothic art changed to more ornamental structure and design; the Limbourg Brothers were Gothic artists

graphic artist – a person who illustrats or designs with a pictorial technique; not interpretive as much as measured and precise; often incorporates and redesigns the art of others through photography and computer techniques

-H-

hatch strokes – in drawing or engraving, little lines made parallel and close together to give the effect of shading; when the lines are crossed over called crosshatching

High Renaissance –
late 1400's-late 1500's
during the late Renaissance and particularly in Northern Europe; a period of art with great attention to realism and detail and making everyday scenes the subject of art work; the most famous High Renaissance painter was Dürer

horizon – the line seen where the sky and the land come together; the word horizontal comes from this term

-I-

illuminated letters – letters in ancient manuscripts and writings that were highly decorated with illustrations or designs in gold, silver, and bright colors, such as found in the Book of Kells; often painted on vellum or parchment (sheets of thin leather used before paper was common)

illuminator – see illuminated letters; usually a monk living and working in a monastery; an artist who made illuminated letters during Medieval times, such as Fra Angelico in 1425

image – any picture, drawing, sculpture, photograph or other form that creates a likeness or representation of an object

imagination – a particularly human trait of being able to think up ideas and dreams and transform them into art

Great Art Words continued

impasto – paints applied in very thick amounts to a canvas or other background

Impressionism, Impressionist – 1860's-19th C.
a major movement and new way of creating art in the late 1800's; painters used natural, free brushwork and painted sunlight into their colors; often showed an impression of reality rather than a perfect life-like report of the subject; some of the most famous Impressionists were Monet, Cassatt, Degas, Renoir, Manet and Morisot

improvisation – a musical term meaning to make up or compose a string of notes which make music; when speaking of art, the artist Kandinsky believed that he could interpret music into abstract art which he called an improvisation

inspiration – the feeling of being motivated or stimulated to create something; to be inspired; an artist may see a beautiful sunset and this then may be the inspiration for a painting with the colors of the sunset

interior design – creating color and design for inside a building; usually involves paint, furniture, art pieces, fabric, tile

inventor – a person who thinks up a new and better way to do something and then designs and often constructs that idea so it may actually work

-J-

junk – items usually thrown away, but in the case of art, collected for uses such as collage, sculpture, assemblage, and other

-K-

kiln – an extremely hot oven for baking clay to a hard and permanent result

-L-

landscape – an art work where the features of the land are the most important subject; usually trees, mountains, rivers, sky, countryside, and so on

Late Gothic – 1330-1450
the end of the Gothic era; ornamentation and height in cathedral design became extreme and elaborate in detail; heavily decorated with jewels, stone work, and painted details; immediately followed by the Renaissance

Louvre – a famous museum in Paris where many of the greatest works of art by the greatest painters of all time are held and displayed

-M-

master – an artist who is known as the teacher or is thought of as the best, as an example to others; a master may also be the training teacher for an apprentice; some of the greatest masters in art history are Da Vinci, Michelangelo, Monet, Botticelli, and El Greco

matte board – a very useful and versatile heavy paper board; available in scraps in a variety of colors and textures, saved from picture frame shops; useful in children's art; can be purchased in large sheets

mixed media – the use of two or more art mediums in an art work; for example, an art work where crayon, paint, and chalk are all used together

mobile – a sculpture that balances, and hangs from the ceiling or hangs from a stand

monastery – many artists of long ago lived and worked in a religious community and were called "Brother" or "Father"; similar to a church with other buildings and grounds where religious people in the group live and work

mono – one; monochrome is one color or tone and monoprint is one image or print

monoprint – when one print is made from one image, rather than many prints from one image

montage – a design not necessarily meant to be an art work; sometimes refers to actors who pose in a still scene to represent a famous painting

monument – a memorial, gravestone or statue to help others remember a person, group of people, important happening, or part of history that is in the past

mosaic – a type of surface decoration used on walls, tables, and walkways where little bits of colored stone or glass are pressed into cement making a design or pattern; in children's art, often refers to less permanent art works made with paper, beans and seeds, egg shells, or other materials

mural – a large painting, often painted on a wall; sometimes painted by more than one person; may be a painting on large canvas or wood panels attached to a wall

muslin – a pure cotton fabric, usually beige or white only, such as a bed sheet

myth – a story that is based in imagination but is believed as if it were fact or history

-N-

Naturalism, Naturalist –
factual and realistic representation in art; the practice of reproducing subjects as exactly as possible; examples are Audubon and Linnaeus

The Nabis – 1891-1900
a group of artists who exhibited together; inspired by Gauguin and his Tahitian paintings that were flat and simple; their style stressed flat lines and

patterns with low-tone colors; often designed costumes and stage sets, illustrated books, and created posters and stained glass; the most famous Nabis painter was Vuillard; known as Post Impressionist

-O-

observe – to look closely; in art, to notice details and record them

optical illusion – an art work where the human eyes and brain work together, where what is seen may appear to move, vibrate, or do things that really are not happening; one of the more famous artists using this technique was Vaserely who made dizzy, wild checkerboard designs

ornate – highly decorative, lavish, and elaborate as in the Baroque Period of art

ornithologist – someone who observes and studies birds; Audubon was an ornithologist who painted pictures of the birds he studied

-P-

palette – any board or tray on which colors are mixed; also refers to the selection of colors an artist choses to paint an art work

papier-mâché – French, meaning mashed paper; one children's art technique is to soak paper strips in wallpaper paste and then cover a form with the strips, later drying to a hard, semi-permanent object

pastel chalk – soft art chalks in many colors

pastels, oil – (Craypas™) a crayon made of ground color (pigments) and mixed with a sticky water or oil; or a drawing made with these coloring sticks

patron – someone who gives an artist money to live on while the artist tries to sell his artworks

pattern – in art a pattern usually means to repeat a design; a pattern can be a single design or stencil that is traced

Great Art Words continued

pediment – a low-pitched triangular area in architecture, formed by the two slopes of a roof and frequently decorated with a sculpture

perspective – a painting or drawing with images and objects that produce an impression of distance and size

photocopy machine – a machine that captures a copy of an image on a piece of paper or document

photocopy – a black and white copy made on a photocopy machine (can also be in color), which can also be enlarged and reduced

photography – (photographer) the art of using a camera and film to capture images; can be expressive or realistic; useful for portraits, landscapes, and all other forms of picture taking

 Photojournalism, Photojournalist – using the art of photography to capture a story, tell a story, or impart history as seen through a camera's lens and developed on photographic paper; Margaret Bourke-White is a famous photojournalist

pigment - the part of paint that is the color; mix piment with egg, water, or other liquid; pigment comes from natural things such as the earth, insects, flowers, or other

 Pointillism, Pointillist – **late 19th C.** **also called Neo-Impressionism** a style of painting developed in France in which pure colors of paint are applied to paper or canvas in small dots; a painting style using dots of color when viewed from a distance, the dots seem to merge and create new colors; the most famous Pointillist is Seurat; a style also used by van Gogh and Toulouse-Lautrec

polymer clay – a plastic based clay such as Fimo™ or Sculpey™ that can be baked hard or reused over and over if not baked; comes in many colors and is highly manageable

Polystyrene™ – grocery tray, a handy material often saved for use in children's art; used for containers for art supplies; foods can be purchased on these trays from grocery stores; come in black, gray, and most often in white in many shapes and sizes

 Pop Art – **1950's-1960's** an art form that used American mass culture and everyday commercial images from foods, cars, and famous people; the two most famous artists of this era were Lichtenstein (who based his art work on comic strips, advertising, and bubble-gum wrappers) and Warhol (who showed soup can labels and movie stars in repetition)

 Pop Op – see Pop Art; added emphasis of optical illusion; Vasarély is famous for his optical illusion art termed Pop Op

portrait – a painting or drawing of a person, sometimes the head and shoulders only, other times the entire body

poster paint – a type of tempera paint

poster – a sheet of paper that advertises or tells and shows information in an artistic way

 Post Impressionism, Post Impressionist – **1880's-1900** an art movement that came after Impressionism; artists tried not to imitate the real world, and created a world of feeling, form, and spirit; typical works had bright colors and splashy brushwork; the most famous Post Impressionists are Cézanne, Gauguin, Van Gogh, Seurat, and Toulouse-Lautrec

pottery – pots, cups, vases, urns, and other containers made from clay and baked hard in a kiln or other oven

primary colors – the basic colors from which all other colors can be made; the primary colors are red, blue, and yellow; mixed in varying ways, these make other colors like green, oragne, purple, and so on

printmaking – any variety of art techniques that involve taking a print of a design, texture, or image with paint, ink, or other art mediums and then pressing it onto another material such as paper to capture the image

prodigy – a child genius or marvel; a child with the talent of an adult

professional training – when an artist is given lessons and instruction in order to become career a professional artist

professional – an artist who is paid for work created and sold

-Q-

-R-

 Realism, Realist – **19th Century c.1848-1860** an era when artists showed life as it really was, including subjects that may not have been popular to show before; for example, Caravaggio painted St. Matthew with dirty feet and Courbet painted a scene involving a funeral; Courbet is the most famous Realist

realistic – when something in art is created to look real, just like it does in actual life

rebirth – a term describing new ideas and new methods in art, music, medicine, and every area of life, particularly in the era of the Renaissance; the French word renaissance means "rebirth"

relief – a sculpture that projects from a background of which it is a part, but is not freestanding

remote control – in the robot sculptures and contraptions of artists like Nam June Paik, the remote control can turn on and off the movement of the sculpture

Renaissance man or Renaissance person – someone who has new ideas and works at implementing them, such as the great Leonardo da Vinci; a term to describe anyone from any time period, ancient or contemporary, who has new thoughts, ideas, and methods

 Renaissance – **c.1200 to 1500** a period of great change in art, architecture, science, medicine, and all areas of creativity and thought; followed the ornate Gothic Period; the 3 greatest Renaissance artists were Leonardo da Vinci, Michelangelo, and Raphael

repetition – duplicating and recurring patterns, designs, or images in an art work

resist – a painting technique where one art medium resists the other; wax resists watercolor paint, for example

 Romanticism, Romantic – **18th C.-19th C. (50 years)** a style of art filled with feelings for nature, emotion and imagination instead of realism or reason, including an interest in the past, the exotic, and the mysterious; famous Romantic artists were Gainsborough and Blake

-S-

scaffold – a platform structure built to reach high places, such as the one Michelangelo used to help him paint the ceiling of the Sistine Chapel

scientist – some artists are also scientists, which helps them invent, draw in detail, or build sculptures that are complicated

Great Art Words continued

Sculpey™ – a commercial clay product that can be easily worked and then baked hard like clay

sculptor – an artist who creates sculptures

sculpture – an art form that is three dimensional, made from any materials, and is usually free-standing

self portrait – a drawing or painting made by the artist of him/herself

series – art works that connect in their subject or design, and are meant to be viewed together, or go together in order

silhouette – an outline style drawing filled in with one color; a shadow or single shape against a background

sketch pad – a pad of drawing paper; the pages are wired or glued together at one edge so they can be torn out

slab of clay – a hunk of clay, usually cut from a larger piece of clay and often in a semi-rectangular or triangular shape; used as the beginning piece from which a clay sculpture is made

stained glass – pieces of colored glass are joined together with a material such as lead to form a design; a picture made with pieces of colored glass statue a sculpture made from any material, usually stone, bronze, or clay; free-standing

still life – objects placed in an arrangement as the subject of a painting

straight edge – any material or object that can be used like a ruler and has a completely straight edge, such as a piece of plastic, the edge of a book, or a paint stirring stick

studio – a room used to make various types of art, such as painting, pottery, clay, and sculpture

Styrofoam™ – white packing material (a by-product of petroleum), very light weight and found in many shapes and textures

surimono – a Japanese form of art used by the artist Hokusai for illustrating greeting cards for special occasions, celebrations, and festivals

 Surrealism, Surrealist, Surreal – 1924-1945 an era of art expressed by fantastic imaginary thoughts and images, often expressing dreams and sub-conscious thoughts as part of reality; illogical and unexpected, surprising imaginary art; followed Dada; the most famous Surrealists are Chagall, Magrit, Oppenheim, and Dali

symmetry – balance or regularity of two sides; one half of something is exactly like the other half

-T-

talk-balloon – a cloud shape next to a character in a cartoon or comic where the words of the character are written to show the character is talking; can be used with inanimate images like a box or a mountain as examples, as well as with people, animals, or creatures

technique – a method or procedure for making art; some common art techniques for children are crayon resist, wet-on-wet painting, and brushed chalk

tempera paint – a common art material found in schools and homes; available in liquid or powdered forms and in many colors; ground pigments sometimes mixed with egg or oil

temple – a building for worship, often with ornate decoration

tessellation, tessela – a design made from shapes that fit together perfectly; a checkerboard is a simple tessellation made of squares; other shapes - such as some triangles, rectangles and diamonds - fit together perfectly in connecting designs; Escher is famous for his tesselations

texture – the quality of the surface of a work of art; for example, rough or smooth; the texture can be felt, seen, or both

three-dimensional (3D) – art work that is solid and has all dimensions: height, width, and depth; not flat; applies to sculptures or works that stand up from a flat surface

trace – place a thin sheet of paper or other material over an art work and draw over it, making the same design or image

transformation – to artistically change or decorate an object or an environment until it is something new, such as the contemporary artist Christo creates; for example, drape orange fabric over a table and chairs so that the objects take on a new shape and are no longer used as a table and chairs

triptych panel – three panels joined together, frequently hinged so that the inner panel is covered when the side panels are closed, such as those created by Fra Angelico

-U-

undulating motion – a rhythm of painting with the brush and hand, such as van Gogh used in his Impressionist painting, *Sunflowers*

Ukiyo-e (Edo Period) – 1615-1857 Ukiyo-e means "pictures of the floating world (everyday life)" school of printmaking; Edo is another name for Tokyo; a period of Japanese printmaking from wood cuts; inspired from traditions, legends, and everyday life of Japanese people; Hokusai and Shunsho are examples of Ukiyo-e artists; well known art example is *Thirty-Six Views of Mount Fuji*, a series of wood block prints

-V-

vellum – a fine parchment made from calfskin and used to write on, such as for illuminated letters and the pages of medieval manuscripts

-W-

wash – a thin, watery mixture of paint, often used over a crayon drawing to resist the crayon and absorb only into the paper; used in watercolor painting, brush drawing, and occasionally in oil painting to describe a broad, thin layer of thinned paint or ink

watercolor – thin, transparent water-soluble paint; comes in children's watercolor boxes, in squeeze tubes, and in dry blocks; when mixed with water thins and is used as paint

waterscape, seascape, or oceanscape – a work of art in which water is the main subject, such as the ocean, the sea, or other bodies of water

wet-on-wet painting – a painting technique where wet paint is applied to wet paper

wood cut, wood print, wood block – a print made by cutting a design in a block of wood and printing only the raised surfaces (not the cut-in areas) on paper

-X-Y-Z-

Great Art Materials

Because art involves saving supplies and materials, this index helps locate a project or activity according to materials on hand. For example, if you have a bouquet of flowers, the index will suggest looking on page 45 for an activity using fresh flowers.

Great Art Materials continued

Jenny Lemon, age 7, Chomp

Great Art Styles

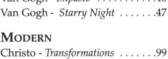

Great Art Techniques

Great artists are listed by the art tecnhique used in the activity and its corresonding page. This list helps locate activity by particular art techniques and art materials on hand.

Great Artist Birthdays

JANUARY
Calder . . . . .January 11, 1889
Morisot . . . . .January 14, 1841
Cézanne . . . . .January 19, 1839
Manet . . . . .January 23, 1832
Pollock . . . . .January 28, 1912

FEBRUARY
Homer . . . . .February 24, 1836
Renoir . . . . .February 25, 1841

MARCH
Michelangelo . . . . .March 6, 1475
Mondrian . . . . .March 7, 1872
Dali . . . . .March 11, 1904
Van Gogh . . . . .March 30, 1853

APRIL
Raphael . . . . .April 6, 1483
Leonardo da Vinci . . . . . . .April 15, 1452
Audubon . . . . .April 26, 1785

MAY
Gainsborough . . . . .May 14, 1727
Dürer . . . . .May 21, 1471
Rousseau . . . . .May 21, 1844
Cassatt . . . . .May 22, 1844

JUNE
Gauguin . . . . .June 7, 1848
Wright . . . . .June 8, 1867
Courbet . . . . .June 10, 1819
Constable . . . . .June 11, 1776
Rubens . . . . .June 28, 1577

JULY
Kahlo . . . . .July 6, 1910
Chagall . . . . .July 7, 1887
Rembrandt . . . . .July 15, 1606
Degas . . . . .July 19, 1834
Moore . . . . .July 30, 1898

AUGUST
Warhol . . . . .August 8, 1930

SEPTEMBER
Arp . . . . .September 16, 1887

OCTOBER
Ringgold . . . . .October 8, 1930
Picasso . . . . .October 25, 1881
Lichtenstein . . . . .October 27, 1923

NOVEMBER
Rodin . . . . November 12, 1840
Monet . . . . November 14, 1840
O'Keeffe . . . . November 15, 1887
Toulouse-Lautrec . . . . November 24, 1864
Blake . . . . November 28, 1757

DECEMBER
Seurat . . . . .December 2, 1859
Kandinsky . . . . .December 4, 1866
Munch . . . . .December 12, 1863
Klee . . . . .December 18, 1879
Matisse . . . . .December 31, 1869

Month and Day Unlisted
Giotto 1266
Ghiberti 1378
Van Eyck 1395
Angelico 1400
Masaccio 1401
Botticelli 1444
El Greco 1541
Linnaeus 1707
Hokusai 1760
Grandma Moses 1860
Russell 1864
Vuillard 1868
Stella 1880
Braque 1882
Rivera 1886
Duchamp 1887
Escher 1889
Lange 1895
Rockwell 1895
Magritte 1898
Nevelson 1900
Giacometti 1901
Cornell 1903
Bourke-White 1906
Smith 1906
Vasarély 1908
Oppenheim 1913
Lawrence 1917
Wyeth 1917
Rauschenberg 1925
Chamberlain 1927
Kienholz 1927
Paik 1932
Christo 1935
Davis 1946
Van Allsburg 1949

Great artists have great birthdays to celebrate from January through December. Some of the artist's birthdays are listed here by month, day, and year. Others, whose months and days were not located, are listed by year only. Have a great art party and celebrate all year long!

Great Artists & Activities

Great artists and their corresponding art activities are listed alphabetically, with page numbers where they can be found.

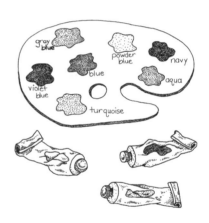

About the Authors & Illustrator

MaryAnn received a BS in Education from Old Dominion University, VA, and a graduate degree from Western Washington University in Elementary Education, English, Speech, and Drama. After teaching primary grades for ten years, MaryAnn retired to raise her family. She is the author of award-winning art books for children, including *Mudworks*, *Scribble Art*, *ScienceArts*, *Preschool Art*, *MathArts*, *Cooking Art*, *Good Earth Art*, and *Discovering Great Artists*. MaryAnn offers workshops and seminars on teaching creatively and using art in the classroom. MaryAnn owns Bright Ring Publishing, Inc. (1985) and lives with her family in Bellingham, Washington.

Kim Solga, a graduate of the University of California at Berkeley, is a nationally acclaimed author and illustrator of children's books. During her varied career, Kim has been an elementary school teacher, a professional artist and stained glass designer, a writer, an internet developer, and the owner of KidsArt, a mail order art supplies catalog for teachers and parents. Her best selling "Arts and Activities" series from NorthLight Publications includes *Draw!*, *Make Prints!*, *Paint!*, and five other titles. Her articles on arts and crafts appear regularly in *Parenting Magazine*, *Child Magazine*, and other education publications. Kim lives in Mt. Shasta, California with her family.

Rebecca Van Slyke is a graduate of Western Washington University in elementary education, who learned to love art from talented and encouraging parents. She has taught grade two at Fisher School in Lynden, Washington for over ten years. Rebecca gives private art lessons to children and writes and illustrates children's books. She lives with her husband, young daughter, and numerous furry and feathered critters on a small farm near Bellingham.

Bright Ideas Bookshelf ••••••• Art Resource Books by MaryAnn F. Kohl ••••••

Process, Not Product Art Series

GREAT AMERICAN ARTISTS FOR KIDS
Hands-On Art Experiences in the Styles of Great American Masters

MaryAnn Kohl & Kim Solga

ISBN 9780935607000

75+ open-ended art ideas focus on the styles of great American masters from colonial times to the present. Full color artworks by masters and children! Young child art options included. Some are Cassatt, Wood, Warhol, Kahn, Hopper, Neiman, Lin, Fish, Chihuly, Hofmann, Stuart, Johns.

$18.95 • 144 pages
Bright Ring • 2008
Ages 4–12

DISCOVERING GREAT ARTISTS
Hands-On Art for Children in the Styles of the Great Masters

MaryAnn Kohl & Kim Solga

ISBN 9780935607093

100+ easy art ideas focusing on the style of a great master from the past or present. More than 80 artists featured including Picasso, Monet, & O'Keeffe. Highly popular art book with numerous awards including Benjamin Franklin and Homeschooling.

$18.95 • 144 pages
Bright Ring • 1996
Ages 3–12

FIRST ART
Art Experienes for Toddlers & Twos

MaryAnn Kohl

ISBN 9780876592229

75+ art experiences are specifically designed for the little guys, including tips for success. Filled with art exploration especially for toddlers and two year olds. *1st book in the Process, Not Product art series.*

$14.95 • 160 pages
Gryphon House • 2002
Ages 1–5

The BIG MESSY ART Book
*But Easy to Clean Up

MaryAnn Kohl

ISBN 9780876592069

100+ adventurous activities beyond the ordinary for exploration of art on a grander more expressive scale. Hundreds of bonus variations included.

$14.95 • 144 pages
Gryphon House • 2000
Ages 4-12

STORYBOOK ART
Hands-On Art for Children in the Styles of 100 Great Picture Book Illustrators

MaryAnn Kohl & Jean Potter

ISBN 9780935607031

100 easy literature based art ideas in the styles of favorite picture book illustrators. Preschool through elementary. Extensive indexes and info.

$18.95 • 144 pages
Bright Ring • 2003
Ages 4–12

MUDWORKS
Creative Clay, Dough and Modeling Experiences

MaryAnn Kohl

ISBN 9780935607024

100+ modeling and play-art ideas using play dough, mud, papier-mâché, plaster of Paris, and other mixtures from household supplies. Award Winning Best Seller. An arts and crafts classic! Voted *Best of the Best.*

$18.95 • 152 pages
Bright Ring • 1989
All Ages

PRESCHOOL ART
It's the Process, Not the Product

MaryAnn Kohl

ISBN 9780876591680

Over 250 process-oriented art projects designed for children 3-6, but enjoyed by kids of all ages. Uses materials found commonly at home or school. Organized by months, seasons, and art techniques. *2nd book in the Process, Not Product art series.*

$24.95 • 260 pages
Gryphon House 1994
Ages 3–6+

COOKING ART

MaryAnn Kohl & Jean Potter

ISBN 9780876591840

150+ artistic, edible recipes for experiencing the joy of food design. Food is designed, prepared and eaten as part of meals, snacks, parties (some for pets and outdoor friends too). Most of the recipes require no cooking or baking.

$19.95 • 160 pages
Gryphon House • 1997
Ages 3–10

SCRIBBLE ART
Independent Creative Art Experiences for Children

MaryAnn Kohl

ISBN 9780935607055

200+ process art ideas that applaud exploring in an independent, non-competitive, open-ended setting. Only basic art materials and kitchen supplies needed. (Originally published as *Scribble Cookies*.) *Scribble Art* is the primer of all Kohl's art books.

$18.95 • 144 pages
Bright Ring • 1994 [1985]
All Ages

MUDWORKS – Bilingüe / Bilingual
Experiencias creativas con arcilla, masa, y modelado
Creative Clay, Dough, and Modeling Experiences

MaryAnn Kohl

ISBN 9780935607178

50+ of the best projects from the original edition of *Mudworks*, translated into both Spanish and English on facing pages, for children and adults of all ages.

$14.95 • 160 pages
Bright Ring • 2002 *Bilingual Edition • Edición bilingüe*

PRIMARY ART
It's the Process, Not the Product

MaryAnn Kohl

ISBN 9780876592830

100+ amazing creative art projects have results to delight and teach elementary aged children. Each activity has three parts: basic, experienced, and challenging. Promote the process of art exploration, and appreciate the individualized result. *3rd book in the Process, Not Product art series.*

$19.95 • 190 pages
Gryphon House • 2005
Ages 5-10

MATH ARTS
Exploring Math through Art for 3-6 Year Olds

MaryAnn Kohl & Cindy Gainer

ISBN 9780876591772

200+ innovative activities to introduce preschoolers through second graders to early math concepts through art projects. Essential math skills without pain!

$24.95 • 260 pages
Gryphon House • 1996
Ages 3–6+

SCIENCE ARTS
Discovering Science Through Art Experiences

MaryAnn Kohl & Jean Potter

ISBN 9780935607048

200+ art experiences explore basic science concepts. Amazing ooo-ahh projects entice even the most reluctant artist into exploration, discovery, and creativity. Projects worthy of repeating over and over.

$18.95 • 144 pages
Bright Ring • 1993
Ages 3–10

GOOD EARTH ART
Environmental Art for Kids

MaryAnn Kohl & Cindy Gainer

ISBN 9780935607017

200+ art explorations using common materials collected from nature or recycled from throw-aways. Filled with easy ideas for appreciating the earth through art.

$18.95 • 224 pages
Bright Ring • 1991
Ages 4–10

GLOBAL ART
Activities, Projects, and Inventions from Around the World

MaryAnn Kohl & Jean Potter

ISBN 9780876591901

135+ easy-to-do art projects exploring collage, painting, drawing, construction, and sculpture while introducing kids to cultures and people worldwide. Activities need only basic art materials and common kitchen supplies.

$16.95 • 190 pages
Gryphon House • 1998
All Ages

MAKING MAKE-BELIEVE
Fun Props, Costumes, & Creative Play Ideas

MaryAnn Kohl

ISBN 9780876591987

125+ ideas for pretend and make-believe through creative art expereinces centered in storybook play, games, cooking, mini-plays, dress-up and masks, imagination spaces, puppets, and more enrich children's playtime.

$16.95 • 190 pages
Gryphon House • 1999
Ages 1–8

PRESCHOOL ART Mini-SERIES
5 books of art fun for preschool kids & older, each book a chapter from the award winning single volume, *Preschool Art.*
64 pages each • 2001 • $9.95

• CLAY & DOUGH	ISBN 9780876592502
• CRAFT & CONSTRUCTION	ISBN 9780876592519
• PAINTING	ISBN 9780876592243
• DRAWING	ISBN 9780876592236
• COLLAGE & PAPER	ISBN 9780876592526